THE LITTLER BOOK OF DARTS

THE LITTLER BOOK OF DARTS

Facts, Stories, Quizzes and Games that Hit the Bullseye

Joe Shooman

bl!nk

First published in the UK in 2025 by Blink Publishing
An imprint of Bonnier Books UK
5th Floor, HYLO, 105 Bunhill Row,
London, EC1Y 8LZ

A CIP catalogue record for this book is available from the British Library.

Paperback ISBN: 9781785128295

Also available as an ebook and an audiobook

1 3 5 7 9 10 8 6 4 2

Design and Typeset by Envy Design Ltd
Printed and bound in Great Britain by Clays Ltd, Elcograf S.p.A.

FSC www.fsc.org
MIX
Paper | Supporting responsible forestry
FSC® C018072

The authorised representative in the EEA is
Bonnier Books UK (Ireland) Limited.
Registered office address: Floor 3, Block 3, Miesian Plaza,
Dublin 2, D02 Y754, Ireland
compliance@bonnierbooks.ie

www.bonnierbooks.co.uk

CONTENTS

INTRODUCTION

Darts. It's the greatest game in the world. No, hang on, that's not right. It's the greatest *sport* in the world. Nope, that's not capturing its utter glory. Let's try again:

Darts is the greatest sport in the *multiverse*.

Like all the best things in life, it's simple on the outside but once you get into it, it's beautifully complex and nuanced. It's one of the great spectator sports, and unlike the top level of professional football, it's still a sport where you feel you can definitely go for a pint with the world champion.

It's had its tough times, its controversies and its outspoken players, but it continues to fascinate millions of people every year. It's a modern phenomenon in many ways but its roots go back for at least a thousand years. Each match has elements of tragedy, triumph, comebacks, psychological battles and even comedy. It's a fast-paced, individual challenge that anyone can participate in. All you need is a set of darts, a board and a dream. Talent obviously helps, but there's no reason you can't enjoy playing on your own just for the hell of it.

Within these pages we track the history of the game, the board, the darts themselves, the players, the controversies and the wonderful moments. Moreover, this book contains many quizzes to tackle, whether you're a newbie to the great game or an experienced dartist. We've also included some practice games, from cricket to noughts and crosses, to keep your mind and throwing arm sharp as the points on your trusted chuckers.

Our walk-on music's starting, we've got our arrows in our top pocket, our shirt is neon and utterly ridiculous, so it's time to get out there and show what we're made of.

THE GREAT DARTS PLAYERS CHALLENGE

Let's start with a little warm-up to get us under way. How much do you know about the current characters bringing this awesome game into the living rooms and hearts of the world (that's via telly and people's subsequent love of the game, they're not literally gonna come round and sit on your sofa wooing you)? Reckon you can beat off all-comers with your knowledge of darts heroes? Here's a quiz to sort out the true oche jockeys from the stage-fright second-prize blaggers as we cover plenty of active darts players.

1. 14th November, 2021. Irish Open Final. Barry Copeland loses 6–2 to whom?

a. Luke Humphries

b. Luke Littler

c. Bobby George

2. And what was the significance of that result?

a. It was Littler's first seniors title

b. Copeland later complained about poor refereeing

c. It was the first ever televised tiebreak

3. What colour was Michael van Gerwen's hair?

a. He's never had any

b. Gingery-brown-dark blond

c. Jet black

4. When did he start to lose his hair?

a. About age 20

b. About age five

c. He hasn't – he shaves for style

5. Anecdotally, why has Luke Humphries got that specific first name?

a. A tribute to the movie *Cool Hand Luke*

b. His dad was a Leeds United fan and it stands for 'Leeds United, Kings (of) Europe'

c. His parents thought he might be a girl so his full name is Lucinda

6. For which county did Humphries' dad play darts?

a. Berkshire

b. Yorkshire

c. Powys

7. It's 17th December, 2019. Ted Evetts has just lost 3–2 in the PDC World Championships. To whom?

a. Steve Beaton

b. John Part

c. Fallon Sherrock

8. And what was the significance of that result?

a. It was the first time a woman had beaten a man at the World Championships

b. It was Beaton's last ever win in a ranked competition

c. It had to be replayed due to an ill-measured oche

9. He's a fan of snakes who was once offered a deal with Glasgow Rangers as a goalkeeper, but became a trainee accountant before taking up professional darts. Who is he?

a. Peter Wright
b. Nathan Aspinall
c. Michael Smith

10. What ailment did that darts player subsequently suffer from in 2022/2023?

a. Gastric flu
b. Twisted ankle
c. Dartitis

11. Who is responsible for the Mohawk haircuts sported by Peter Wright?

a. His wife, Jo, a hairdresser
b. His personal stylist, Big Les
c. He does it himself

12. Where does Snakebite come from?

a. Manchester, England
b. Livingston, Scotland
c. Bangor, Wales

13. How about Stephen 'The Bullet' Bunting – where's his hometown?

a. Liverpool
b. Ullapool
c. Pontypool

14. What happened on 12th January, 2014 to delight The Bullet?

a. He won the BDO World Championship
b. He qualified as a professional
c. He made his debut at Anfield in an exhibition

15. Why does Rob Cross have the nickname 'Voltage'?

a. He is electric to watch
b. He once worked as an electrician
c. He once got struck by lightning

16. Tuesday, 28th December, 2022. Cross vs Daryl Gurney. What was special about the match?

a. It's the first time the players, who are cousins, played each other on TV
b. Daryl Gurney changed his darts halfway through the match
c. Rob won the match with a 170 checkout

17. This Aussie marvel only started playing seriously aged 15 when his parents were short of a player for their team. Who is he?

a. Josh Rock
b. Danny Noppert
c. Damon Heta

18. He and Simon Whitlock did what in June, 2022?

a. Won the World Cup of Darts for Australia
b. Went skiing across Scandinavia for charity
c. Had a head-to-head battle that ended 22–21

19. How did Jonny Clayton get his nickname 'The Ferret'?

a. He works part-time as a pest removal officer
b. When he played rugby as a nipper he was very skinny
c. He is a fan of Oasis and people say he's 'mad ferret'

20. Aside from darts, what does Clayton do?

a. Works as a plasterer
b. Works as an exterminator
c. Works in an off-licence

21. What put paid to Dave Chisnall's dreams of being a pro footballer?

a. A broken foot aged 17 while playing in St Helens
b. A lack of any discernible talent
c. He argued with the youth team manager and was sacked

22. What award did he win in 2012?

a. Greatest walk-on music
b. Best PDC Newcomer
c. Most Improved BDO Player

23. How did Chris Dobey apparently get his nickname 'Hollywood'?

a. He once wore a baseball cap during a match as an amateur
b. He used to talk in interviews with a Los Angeles accent
c. He was an extra in *Home Alone III: Alone At Home*

24. From where does Chris hail?

a. Bedlington, Northumberland
b. Bedford, Bedfordshire
c. Scunthorpe, Lincolnshire

25. James 'The Machine' Wade is often known as what?

a. The best-ever left-handed player
b. The best-ever player with glasses
c. The most stylish player on tour

26. He has been on the receiving end of what record?

a. The biggest number of 180s in a match
b. The biggest number of nine-darters by his opponents
c. The most losses by a single leg in tournaments

27. Hooker for Neath and Cross Keys. Player with South Wales Scorpions and Blackwood Bulldogs. Capped by Wales Dragonhearts. Which darts legend are we talking about?

a. Gerwyn Price
b. Leighton Rees
c. Richie Burnett

28. What bizarre piece of kit was that player sporting during the 2023 World Darts Championships?

a. A rugby helmet
b. A set of ear defenders
c. An enormous plastic codpiece

29. From rugby to Rocky . . . this new player on the scene gained his tour card through Q-School in 2022. Who is he?

a. John Rambo
b. James Rockett
c. Josh Rock

30. And who did he defeat in the 2024 Dutch Darts Championship by 8–4 to win his first PDC European Tour Title?

a. Jonny Clayton
b. Gerwyn Price
c. Luke Littler

31. Gary Anderson is nicknamed 'The Flying Scotsman' – but what is the original *Flying Scotsman*?

a. An aeroplane
b. A jet pack
c. A steam train

32. What nationality is Danny Noppert?

a. English
b. Belgian
c. Dutch

33. Among other feats, what specifically did this legend achieve in 2015 and 2016?

a. Back-to-back PDC World Championships
b. Undefeated for two seasons
c. Didn't lose a leg in his European Championship games

34. And what is Noppert's nickname?

a. The Heat
b. The Freeze
c. The Juice

35. Who did Dimitri van den Bergh defeat 8–4 in the 2020 World Matchplay Final?

a. Luke Humphries
b. Gary Anderson
c. Josh Rock

36. And who did he defeat 11–10 in a storming 2024 UK Open Final?

a. Luke Humphries
b. Gary Anderson
c. Josh Rock

37. Who did Ross Smith lose 5–1 to in the 2011 quarter-finals of the BDO World Championships?

a. Gary Anderson
b. Martin Adams
c. Bobby George

38. And from which English county does Smudger hail?

a. Devon
b. Wiltshire
c. Kent

39. Surely this is simple – from where does Ricardo Pietreczko get his nickname?

a. A Japanese card/video game
b. A Spanish chain of restaurants
c. A German cartoon series about ants

40. You'd go to his home town the morning after the night before, perhaps. Where?

a. Recovery, Austria
b. Hanover, Germany
c. Alka-Seltzer, Switzerland

41. What's notable about 'Rapid' Ricky Evans' darts?

a. At 19g, they're on the lighter side

b. They're all different colours

c. At 40g, they're the heaviest on the circuit

42. Which seasonal singalong has Evans walked out to on occasion?

a. Slade: 'Merry Xmas Everybody'

b. Paul McCartney: 'Wonderful Christmastime'

c. Shakin' Stevens: 'Merry Christmas Everyone'

43. What happened to the runner-up trophy of the 2016 International Darts Open?

a. It was lost after a rowdy after-party at Gerwyn Price's rugby club

b. Kim Huybrechts trashed it after losing 6–5 to Mensur Suljović

c. It had to be taken back to be re-ground after it was spelled 'rubbers up'

44. At which unusual darts event did Kim represent Belgium in the EDF European Championships?

a. The 2017 Men's Cricket

b. The 2015 Killer Knockout

c. The 2020 Men's Poker

45. The 2021 Players Championship Finals. Peter Wright 11–10 . . . who?

a. Josh Rock
b. Stephen Bunting
c. Ryan Searle

46. What eye condition does that player live with?

a. Short-sightedness
b. Astigmatism
c. Long-sightedness

47. He hit a nine-darter in his winning PDC World Championship Final, 2023. Who is he?

a. Ryan Searle
b. Michael Smith
c. Martin Adams

48. Who was his partner in the 2024 World Cup of Darts win for England?

a. Luke Littler
b. Luke Humphries
c. Dave Chisnall

49. He hails from Strausberg, Germany, and won his PDC tour card through 2017's Q-School. Who is he?

a. Martin Schindler

b. Gabriel Clemens

c. Ricardo Pietreczko

50. He's nicknamed 'The Real Deal' but should really be called 'Blacken' – who's this player?

a. Raymond van Barneveld

b. Mike De Decker

c. Derek Dick

'Phil Taylor's got the consistency of a planet – and he's in a darts orbit.'

DARTS CALENDAR

Note that all events are subject to change so double-check before booking your table at the venue, otherwise you might end up cheering on Mrs Gagsonit vs Old Mother Huckleberry at the World Crocheting Championships. Where dates and venues were not available at the time of press, we've placed events based on when they happened in 2025 (as per PDC/WDF listings). So be sure to double-top, we mean double-check, with your favourite sources online and in the Yellow Pages (ask your great-grandad). Ta, chums.

'There's only one word for that: magic darts!'

Date	Event	Venue/Location
January		
04/01/2026	WDF Pacific Masters Youth/ Girls 2026	Club Forster, NSW, Australia
	Las Vegas Open/Las Vegas Classic	Las Vegas, USA
	Snoflake Open	Canada
	Fire on the Mountain	USA
	Romanian Open/Romanian Classic	Romania
	UK Qualifying School	Milton Keynes, UK
	European Qualifying School	Kalkar, Germany
	Bahrain Darts Masters	Bahrain
	Winmau Challenge Tour	Milton Keynes, UK
	Ladbrokes UK Open Amateur Qualifiers	Milton Keynes, UK
	Toto Dutch Darts Masters	Den Bosch, Netherlands
	Winmau World Masters Prelims	Milton Keynes, UK
	Winmau World Masters	Milton Keynes, UK
February		
5–8/2/26	WDF Dutch Open 2026	De Bonte Wever, Assen, Netherlands

Date	Event	Venue/Location
19–21/2/26	World Seniors Darts Championship	Purfleet, UK
	Canterbury Classic	New Zealand
	South Australian Classic	Australia
	Scottish Open/Scottish Classic	Scotland
	Slovak Open/Slovak Masters	Slovakia
	Port City Open	USA
	BetMGM Premier League	Belfast
	Ladbrokes UK Open Qualifiers	Wigan, UK
	Players Championship	Wigan, UK
	ET 1–2 Tour Card Holder Qualifiers	Wigan, UK
	BetMGM Premier League	Glasgow, UK
	Women's Series	Leicester, UK
	Players Championship	Rosmalen, Netherlands
	ET 1–2 Tour Card Holder Qualifiers	Rosmalen, Netherlands
	BetMGM Premier League	Dublin, Ireland
	Winmau Development Tour	Milton Keynes, UK
	BetMGM Premier League	Exeter, UK
	Ladbrokes UK Open	Butlin's Minehead, UK

Date	Event	Venue/Location
March		
14–15/3/26	International WDF Youth Challenge	Kulturgarage Seestadt Aspern, Vienna, Austria
14–15/3/26	WDF IYC Vienna Masters 2026	Kulturgarage Seestadt Aspern, Vienna, Austria
	NSW Great Lakes Open	New South Wales, Australia
	Winter Special/Winter Classic	Hungary
	Isle of Man Classic/Isle of Man Masters	Isle of Man, UK
	West Coast Classic	Western Australia
	Missouri St Patrick's Day Open	Missouri, USA
	Virginia Beach Classic	Virginia Beach, USA
	AB Darts Open	Canada
	BetMGM Premier League	Brighton, UK
	Lecot Belgian Darts Open	Belgium
	Women's Series	Leicester, UK
	Players Championship	Leicester, UK
	BetMGM Premier League	Nottingham, UK
	Winmau Challenge Tour	Hildesheim, Germany

Date	Event	Venue/Location
	Players Championship	Hildesheim, Germany
	BetMGM Premier League	Cardiff, UK
	Elten Safety Shoes European Darts Trophy	Göttingen, Germany
	BetMGM Premier League	Newcastle, UK
	Winmau Development Tour	Leicester, UK
April		
	White Mountain Shootout	USA
	Torshavn Open/Faroe Islands Darts Open	Faroe Islands
	Budapest Classic/Budapest Masters	Hungary
	Estonia Open/Tallinn Open	Latvia
	South Island Masters	Australia
	Victorian Easter Classic	Australia
	Scottish Easter Singles	Scotland
	Murray Bridge Grand Prix	Australia
	Manitoba Open	Canada
	Salmon Harvest Open	Canada
	Tricoda Open	USA
	Spring Special Darts Open	Hungary
	Iceland Open/Iceland Masters	Iceland

Date	Event	Venue/Location
	North Island Masters	Australia
	Margie O'Donohue Memorial	USA
	Players Championship	Leicester, UK
	ET5–6 Tour Card Holder Qualifiers	Leicester, UK
	BetMGM Premier League	Berlin, Germany
	Elten Safety Shoes International Darts Open	Riesa, Germany
	Players Championship	Leicester, UK
	BetMGM Premier League	Manchester, UK
	Women's Series	Rosmalen, Netherlands
	Players Championship	Rosmalen, Netherlands
	Bet MGM Premier League	Rotterdam, Netherlands
	German Darts Grand Prix	Munich, Germany
	BetMGM Premier League	Liverpool, UK
	Elten Safety Shoes Austrian Darts Open	Graz, Austria
May		
	Denmark Open/Denmark Masters	Denmark
	Cleveland Extravaganza	USA

Date	Event	Venue/Location
	Silver Classic	Australia
	Cyprus Classic/Cyprus Masters	Cyprus
	Selangor Open	Selangor, Malaysia
	Mongolian Open/ Ulaanbaatar Open	Ulaanbaatar, Mongolia
	Canadian Open (Youth)	Canada
	Hutt Valley Singles	Australia
	Vilnius Open/Lithuanian Open	Lithuania
	Sunshine State Classic	Australia
	Spring Classic Darts Open	Hungary
	England Youth Grand Prix Open	UK
	Toronto Area Open/Toronto Area Classic	Toronto, Canada
	Helvetia Open/Swiss Open	Helvetia, Switzerland
	Geelong Dart Club Classic	Geelong, Australia
	BetMGM Premier League	Birmingham, UK
	Winmau Challenge Tour	Milton Keynes, UK
	Elten Safety Shoes European Darts Grand Prix	Sindelfingen, Germany
	BetMGM Premier League	Leeds, UK
	Winmau Development Tour	Hildesheim, Germany

Date	Event	Venue/Location
	ET7–8 Tour Card Holder Qualifiers	Hildesheim, Germany
	BetMGM Premier League	Aberdeen, UK
	BetMGM Premier League	Sheffield, UK
	Dutch Darts Championship	Rosmalen, Netherlands
	Bet MGM Premier League Playoffs	London, UK
	European Darts Open	Leverkusen, Germany
June		
	Canterbury Open	Canterbury, Australian
	England Open/England National Singles	UK
	IYC Hungary/WDF Youth Challenge	Hungary
	Finnish Open/Finnish Masters	Finland
	Cherry Bomb International	USA
	New Zealand Open	New Zealand
	Canadian Open	Canada
	Danube Classic/Danube Masters	Hungary

Date	Event	Venue/Location
	England Youth Grand Prix Open	UK
	Mr Vegas Nordic Darts Masters	Copenhagen, Denmark
	Women's Series	Milton Keynes, UK
	BetVictor World Cup of Darts	Frankfurt, Germany
	Players Championship	Leicester
	ET9–10 Tour Card Holder Qualifiers	Leicester
	bet365 US Darts Masters	New York, USA
July		
	Japan Open/Bud Brick Memorial	Japan
	New Zealand Youth Open	New Zealand
	England Youth Grand Prix Masters	UK
	WDF Europe Cup Youth	Netherlands
	Pacific Masters	Australia
	Music City Classic	USA
	England Youth Grand Prix Classic	UK
	Superbet Poland Darts Masters	Gliwice, Poland

Date	Event	Venue/Location
	Players Championship	Leicester, UK
	Baltic Sea Darts Open	Kiel, Germany
	Betfred World Matchplay/ Women's World Matchplay	Blackpool, UK
	Players Championship	Hildesheim, Germany
	ET11–12 Tour Card Holder Qualifiers	Hildesheim, Germany
August		
	Antwerp Open/Belgium Open	Belgium
	International WDF Youth Challenge	Denmark
	Betty Hislop State Youth Singles	Australia
	IYC Denmark Masters	Denmark
	Timișoara International Darts Open/Grand Prix	Romania
	USA Darts Open/Darts Classic	USA
	Swedish Open/Swedish Masters	Sweden
	International WDF Youth Challenge/Masters	Germany
	Summer Special Darts Open	Hungary
	Malaysian Open	Malaysia

Date	Event	Venue/Location
	England Youth Grand Prix Special	UK
	Welsh Open/Welsh Classic	UK
	Washington Area Open	USA
	New Zealand Masters	New Zealand
	Carinthian Mountain Darts/ Juniors	Austria
	KenoGO Australian Darts Masters	Australia
	New Zealand Darts Masters	Auckland, New Zealand
	Winmau Challenge Tour	Leicester, UK
	Women's Series	Milton Keynes, UK
	Players Championship	Milton Keynes, UK
	Jack's World Series of Darts Finals Tour Card Holder Qualifier	Milton Keynes, UK
	Flanders Darts Trophy	Antwerp, Belgium
September		
	Lower Austrian Masters/ Death Angel Open	Austria
	Catalonia Open	Catalonia
	England Youth Grand Prix Challenge	UK
	Witch City Open	USA

Date	Event	Venue/Location
	Summer Classic	Hungary
	Italian Open/Italian Grand Masters	Italy
	Taranaki Open	New Zealand
	British Open/British Classic	UK
	North Queensland Classic	Australia
	Johor Open	Malaysia
	WDF World Cup/Korean Open	South Korea
	Winmau Development Tour	Wigan, UK
	Czech Darts Open	Prague, Czech Republic
	Players Championship	Hildesheim, Germany
	ET13–14 Tour Card Holder Qualifiers	Hildesheim, Germany
	Jack's World Series of Darts Finals	Amsterdam, Netherlands
	Hungarian Darts Trophy	Hungary
	Swiss Darts Trophy	Switzerland
	Players Championship	Leicester, UK
October		
	Bruges Open/Belfry Open	Belgium
	Savaria Masters/Savaria Classic	Hungary

Date	Event	Venue/Location
	Klondike Open	Canada
	England Masters/England Classic	UK
	Bunbury Classic	Australia
	Auckland Open/Pit to Port Classic	New Zealand
	Thunder Bay Open	Canada
	Latvian Open/Riga Open	Riga, Latvia
	Scary Hare	USA
	Victorian Classic	Australia
	Hungarian Masters/ Hungarian Classic	Hungary
	Alan King Memorial	New Zealand
	Scottish Autumn Singles	UK
	World Open/World Masters	Hungary
	Players Championship	Leicester, UK
	BoyleSports World Grand Prix	Leicester, UK
	Winmau Development Tour	Wigan, UK
	Winmau World Youth Championship Early Rounds	Wigan, UK
	Players Championship	Wigan, UK
	German Darts Championship	Hildesheim, Germany
	Women's Series	Wigan, UK

Date	Event	Venue/Location
	Machineseeker European Championship	Dortmund, Germany
	Winmau Challenge Tour	Wigan, UK
	Players Championship	Wigan, UK
	Mr Vegas Grand Slam of Darts Tour Card Holder Qualifier	Wigan, UK
November		
	Newcastle Classic	Australia
	World Championship Qualifiers	Netherland
	Irish Open/Irish Classic	Ireland
	Slovenia Masters/Slovenia Open	Slovenia
	Malta Open/Malta Masters	Malta
	Seacoast Open	USA
	Ted Clements Memorial	New Zealand
	Czech Open	Czech Republic
	IYC Masters/Youth Challenge	Malta
	WDF World Championships	UK
	Mr Vegas Grand Slam of Darts	Wolverhampton, UK
	Ladbrokes Players Championship Finals	Butlin's Minehead, UK

Date	Event	Venue/Location
	Winmau World Youth Championship Final	Butlin's Minehead, UK
	Paddy Power World Darts Championship Tour Card Holder Qualifier	Leicester, UK
December		
	Borealis Quest	USA
	Xmas Classic	Australia
	Laketown Open/Christmas Special	Austria
	PDC World Darts Championship	London, UK

'Even Hypotenuse would have trouble working out these angles.'

'There's no one quicker than these two tungsten tossers.'

'Phil Taylor went to see a psychologist and was told if he wants to get psyched up, he should listen to Oasis. I reckon darts fans will get a Tungsten Supernova.'

QUIZ

DARTS 101

We all have to start somewhere – and a working knowledge of the basic gear, rules, plus the ins and outs of the great game of darts is advisable, if not totally essential, to getting stuck in. Here's a quick quiz-let to assist you in making that first step towards an inevitable World Championship win in about, oh, let's say six months. That should be more than enough time for you to get your skills up to speed, surely? Game on . . .

1. In most major tournaments, from which score do the players usually begin?

a. 501
b. 101
c. 301

2. What's the name of the line or little raised area behind which players must stand to throw?

a. Bullseye
b. Oche
c. Flight Deck

3. Complete this phrase: 'Let's . . . Darts!'

a. Watch
b. Deliver
c. Play

4. What's the maximum score a player can get in three darts?

a. 200
b. 180
c. 170

5. If a player hits 'double top', how much have they scored?

a. 40
b. 50
c. Zero with two darts

6. How many different single numbers are there on a standard dartboard? (Clue: not all of them actually show their number.)

a. 20
b. 21
c. 25

7. What is a 'bounce-out'?

a. When a player is kicked out of the game for foul language and forfeits the match
b. When a fan is escorted from the premises by door staff for being too drunk
c. When a dart hits the board but does not stick, literally 'bouncing out' and landing on the floor

8. What is a 'bogey'?

a. When a player uses a dart to pick their nose and shows everybody the green stuff

b. When a player is on a score under 170 that cannot be completed in three darts

c. When a game has to be postponed at the last minute due to a rail replacement bus

9. What is a 'flight' in darts terms?

a. The trajectory a dart takes on its way to the board

b. The winged part of the dart that allows it to fly through the air

c. The area of the stage in which a darts game is played

10. Why might a player be given 'no score'?

a. Either they have missed the board with three darts, or they have scored higher than their finishing total

b. They are late for the game and have been penalised by the match referee

c. The players, instead of having a game of 501, have agreed to disagree and have a pint instead

11. What is 'bust' in a darts context?

a. Usually when a player is on a finish and scores more than their total
b. When a player has lost in the first round and must pay a fee to organisers for poor play
c. When a player is considered an idol of the game they are given their own statue

12. When a dart hits the outer ring of a number, what happens?

a. It doubles that dart's score, so the outer ring of 20 is 40
b. It doubles their total score during that game
c. Nothing – it is there to strengthen the board

13. Why do players often try and set up a finish on double 16?

a. It is the closest number to the throwing action of most players
b. If you hit a single, it is the number that can be halved the most
c. It is a traditional initiation into the World Championships

14. What is the significance of 170?

a. It is the lowest high score with three darts

b. It is the highest three-dart finish

c. It is the only prime number on the board

15. What is a 'checkout'?

a. When a darts player comes and tries out the board before a match

b. When a player is knocked out of a tournament

c. When a player gets their score to 0 and wins

16. What are legs, sets and matches?

a. The different stages of a competition match, roughly equivalent to games, sets and matches in tennis

b. They are all different names for a game of darts depending which country you are playing in

c. They all mean the same thing but over the years have become obsolete

17. What is a darts 'bed'?

a. The last game of a match

b. The scoring area of a number

c. The item in which a player stores their darts

18. Bit tougher, this: what is 'mad house'?

a. When the players are really riled up and chucking darts willy-nilly

b. When there is only five minutes left to play so everyone speeds up

c. Another term for double 1 – the lowest double available

19. What does PPD stand for?

a. Points Per Dart, i.e. average score per dart

b. Perfect Player Darts, i.e. a nine-dart finish

c. Prize Point Darts, i.e. a winning visit

20. Which phrase might you hear when you hit the winning double?

a. 'That's Darts!'

b. 'Great Shot'

c. 'Game Shot'

SID WADDELL: THE VOICE OF DARTS

2ND AUGUST, 1940–11TH AUGUST, 2012

One of the greatest heroes darts has ever produced isn't a player at all.

In fact, the legend we speak of had been a noted social studies academic, a trade union expert, a folk singer and a television news producer before going anywhere near the great game of arrows.

We refer, of course, to the peerless Sidney Waddell – a commentator whose one-liners and colourful interjections combined sheer joy of the game with an extremely sharp intellect, melding historical references with moments of darting pain and glory.

It could all have been so different, however, had the Cambridge graduate not been injured playing for his university's rugby second XV. Sid, famously the son of a Northumberland miner (he hails from Alnwick), got to Cambridge on a scholarship. However, that rugby injury turned him towards a less painful sport – darts – where he was responsible for organising an intra-college challenge contest. His team of St John's College came second to, as history's mischievous shenanigans had it, a team of vicars in training.

After graduation, Waddell bounced around various different jobs, one being a folk duo called the Gravy-boatmen; however, it was the small screen that finally drew him into the fold and he began working for Granada TV. After a couple of years alongside the likes of future TV chat-show host Michael Parkinson, Waddell jumped across the Pennines to work for Yorkshire TV's daily news show, *Calendar*.

Darts Beckons

News just didn't have enough of a narrative for our Sid, though, and after watching the 1972 *News of the World* darts championships at Ally Pally, he went back to Yorkshire with the idea of a show called *Indoor League*. The programme broadcast various different pubs competing at the vast amount of pub games available at the time. Given it was several decades before Sky TV and computers, people passed their hours drinking stinking ale out of pint pots with handles, and testing their mettle at the likes of billiards, skittles, shove ha'penny (ask yer grandad) and even arm-wrestling. It also, of course, featured darts, as pubs up and down the region all had room for a board, and all had their local champions too.

Indoor League is still broadcast to this day on various satellite channels and is an absolutely immense slice of local history – Waddell may not have intended to make a cultural time capsule, but if you seek out episodes online you'll see the fashions, prices, accents, and lots and lots of people smoking pipes, that make the past a truly fascinating place.

By 1976 Sid had moved to the BBC and became one of the most iconic commentators of all time. As well as his work on all the Beeb's darts events, he produced various shows for kids and adults including the equally iconic football show, *Jossy's Giants*, which he also wrote.

Wahey, Sky

The advent of Sky TV tended to hoover up sports and sports commentators alike, and by 1994 Waddell was most often seen and heard on tournaments covered by that massive satellite-based company. Darts itself was becoming ever-more glamorous, the prizes bigger and bigger, and the profile and the skills of the players followed suit. A golden age for darts and darts fans with the glitz and showmanship more akin to a boxing match; with dancing girls, fireworks, walk-ons, excellent sound systems and loud music, it was miles away from the staid, brown-ale guzzling men in flat caps of only two decades earlier. Waddell also commentated on pool, hosted a wrestling show and worked with Eric Bristow to repackage classic darts matches for ESPN.

A successful screenwriter, his cricket show *Sloggers* gained him a nomination for Best Screenwriter for the 1994 Writers' Guild of Great Britain awards, and he also published 11 books including biographies of darts legends like Phil Taylor, plus a 2009 memoir. Oh, and a red-hot novel about a Geordie groupie – released in 1973, *Bedroll Bella* had the dubious accolade of being banned by high street stores John Menzies and WHSmith. Always a great way to bring the sales in!

Sadly, Waddell died of bowel cancer on 11th August, 2012, aged 72. The PDC World Darts Championship trophy is now named the Sid Waddell Trophy – testament to a man whose humble beginnings and rise to the very top of his game is the kind of rags-to-riches story that itself deserves a biopic. Woe betide he or she who tries to write his dialogue, though – the man was a complete one-off.

Throughout this book you will find many of his wonderful, eccentric one-liners and quotes. As the man himself said: 'There's only one word to describe that: magic darts.'

'Once upon a time he was breaking all records, now he's only breaking his hearts. Nothing you can do, total eclipse of the dart.'

QUIZ

ON THE OCHE

It's a vital piece of the darting set-up but technically you don't need anything physical at all. It's there to keep everyone in line, or at least behind it. You can chuck your arrows from anywhere behind it – yes, folks, it's the oche, and without it there would be chaos. All hail our oche overlord! How much do you know about it?

1. In standard steel-tip darts, how far away from the board is the oche?

a. Ten feet from the top of the board to the oche, diagonally

b. Nine feet and seven and three-eighth inches from the bullseye to the oche, diagonally

c. Ten feet from the unclothed midriff of the nearest cheerleader, diagonally

2. How many of the player's feet must touch the oche?

a. None

b. One

c. Two

3. Which of these definitions is a possible origin story for the word 'oche'? Note that there may be more than one correct answer, so you may choose as many or as few as you like. A point for each correct answer – but a point off for every incorrect one, so don't just pick 'em all and hope for the best!

a. It is an Old-English version of the modern word 'OK', and was said when a player was an acceptable distance from the board to take their turn

b. It is derived from an Old-English word ‘hocken’, as in ‘hocking up a greenie’ (to spit). Before darts was popular, spitting contests in pubs were regular occurrences
c. It was coined by legendary commentator Sid Waddell, a history graduate, and based on an Ancient Greek word *okkus*, meaning ‘tree branch’
d. The distance from the board was once measured in beer crates from a West-Country brewer called ‘S Hockey and Sons’
e. The word is derived from an Old Flemish word which means something like ‘notch’ or ‘a nick’, reflecting the fact that often a notch was scarred in the wooden floors to designate the throwing line
f. It is from Middle French. The word ‘oche’ comes from an Old French word *ochier* meaning ‘to make a notch in’

GAME

Would I lie to my friends?

Another magnificent and totally original format that we’ve literally just made up and anyone who says anything else is, well, a liar. We're basing this example on Question Three above – the origins of the word 'oche' – but obviously you can make up a game from any source material you choose, you crazy apes.

Two-player game

Each player picks a definition *without knowing whether it is true or not.* They must convince their friend that the definition is true. Player Two guesses True or False. A point for a correct answer.

Each player can pick two definitions each, and take it in turn as above. Do not look at the answers until each player has had two turns! The winner is the one with the most correct answers. Points off for an incorrect guess.

Multiplayer game: version one

One player picks a definition and has to convince all the other players that it is true. A point to each player who guesses correctly, and a point taken off those who are incorrect. As there are six definitions here, this can go for six rounds – either with the same player convincing everyone else, or each player having a turn in the hot seat. If it is a single person doing all the convincing, they are playing against all the others for points. In the other version, it's each player for themselves.

In the single-convincer version, that player alone can check if the actual answer is true or false, but nobody else may. If you play with a moving hot seat where everyone has a go, nobody may check the answer until all rounds are finished.

Multiplayer game: version two

Make two teams. One player picks a definition and convinces the other team, as above. The player's teammates can back up their fact-telling person, or cast suspicious light on it, perhaps in a double bluff.

A point to the guessing team, if they are correct; a point off, if not; a point to the convincer's team if they successfully fool their opponents.

Multiplayer quiz challenge

Nominate one person as quiz-meister – you'll have to give them a day or a week's advance notice here. The quiz-meister then researches (for example) 12 questions in the vein of our oche example, and is the only person that holds the information as to what is correct or incorrect.

You can play this with any number of players including teams – as in multiplayer game: version two – or as individuals in a knockout FA Cup-style manner. That is, pair up players into guesser and convincer, and they are knocked out either when someone guesses correctly (knocking out the convincer), or the guesser gets it wrong and the convincer goes through to the next round.

If you are the quiz-meister, make sure your answers are clear and you can reference them – there's gonna be some arguments here . . .

'That was delicate, like a surgeon near a delicate area.'

PLAY IT: 501

GAME

Players:

One or more

In brief:

Get that score down to zero – but you must finish on a double (usually).

How to play:

First decide who goes first: closest to bull, coin toss, quickest pint downed, alphabetical order, *Squid Game*, soggy biscuit, etc. Then take it in turns to chuck your three darts at the round thing. Use maths to subtract numbers hit from numbers written on the chalkboard. Keep going until someone zeroes (checks out) their score via a double of any kind, including the bull. If you're on a checkout, but go over your score, then your darts in that visit are void. So, if you need 40 (double top), and hit 20 on your first dart then for some reason hit double top with your second then your notional score of 60 is nullified and your visit is over. Your score reverts to 40 needed for your next visit.

It's the big kahuna this one: the standard for virtually all darts matches on telly. Take it in turns to go first. The overall game might be a straight shoot-out, i.e. first to win 19 single visits (legs), or based on the amount of sets won. A set is generally scored over the best of three (first to two) or the best of five (first to three). The winner of the match would be the first to, for example, 10 sets (aka best of 19). 501 is a game that stretches all darts skills: you may be a very heavy scorer with an average of 100 or more, but if you can't hit the doubles you're never going to win a game. Similarly, if you're a fiendish hitter of the doubles but can't score for toffee, you may never get a chance to get to the doubles in the first place. And you certainly won't win any toffee either, we're sorry to report. Either way, the fewest darts you can use is a slinky nine, which is why nine-darters are so celebrated when someone nails one. Ultimately, though, whether you've stuck a nine-darter or ground out the leg over 26 darts, you will still only score one leg. Trebles for play, doubles for pay may be a cliché but it's a cliché for a reason: 'cause it's true.

Variation one

Start and finish with a double, which quite frankly is absolutely irritating and not worth it because if you want to practise doubles then practise doubles rather than sticking one in at the beginning of a game when you're all geared up to smack out some sweet trebles. Note that when you double in, as it's called, any darts thrown before you hit a double are non-scorers. So, if player one hits 3, D6, T20 then the score is 72, not 75, as that initial single 3 does not count. If you're playing a versus game that involves teams then you can choose if any double by any of your players frees the rest to score, or if each player on each team must double in to be an active (scoring) player.

Variation two

Start at 301, or 1001, or 101, or 9,000,001. Any number you choose. The element of competition against another player is as important as the number you start with, really.

But why 501?

If it was 500, setting up doubles would be as easy as just hanging around in the 20s bed, and nobody would ever learn how to switch to other numbers as a result.

NO NEED TO GET SHIRTY: DRESSING FOR SUCCESS . . . OR NOT

From the truly minging to the borderline ridiculous, the shirts darts players wear onstage are nothing if not recognisable. Their attire may seem like the aftermath of a free-for-all trolley dash around a particularly garish garment warehouse where all the lighting has been broken for years, but there's actually nearly always method behind the sartorial madness.

Indeed, there's a whole bunch of PDC rules to adhere to when considering which shirts to wear onstage, one being that each player must bring two different colour shirts to an event. This is so the tournament director can check them for things like advertising regulations, colour clashes with players of a higher rank and a whole bunch of other stuff. Brilliantly, if the tourney boss or the PDC reckon neither shirt fulfils the required criteria, said player will be issued a plain shirt for that match by the PDC itself. This, for the avoidance of doubt, is the equivalent of having to do PE in your pants and socks if you forget your kit. (Other regs state that smart trousers and footwear must be worn – jeans and 'casual trousers' are prohibited, as are trainers.)

Fortunately, however, the get-out clause also exists that up until four hours before a match begins, a player can petition the tournament director to wear different clothes – this is how someone like Peter Wright manages to come onstage dressed as The Grinch, for example. So it's quite flexible in practice, up to a point.

Rules and rules

Logos and ads are, however, restricted to certain places on the shirts and up to five different ones can be worn, plus two that the PDC issue for the match. In total, each advertising logo can't exceed 40cm square, including the background. Makers' logos (like a Nike swoosh) must be covered up unless a player has a specific endorsement with the brand, and even then that space must be covered by a patch from the sponsor.

When it comes to players' own branding – their names, or a lightning fork, or whatever – the rules aren't as strict, although the PDC does specify 'in moderation' for them. The reason players wear the synthetic shirts? Not really for comfort – although a cotton shirt can get really heavy under the studio lights so those are best avoided anyway – but simply because polyester, for example, can be printed using sublimation techniques, which makes them simple and cheap to reproduce for replicas.

If you're Gerwyn Price, of course, you're going to look buff AF in anything, but a too-tight playing shirt is not such a good idea if you're, let's say, on the generously stomached side. A tight shirt restricting blood flow to your arms is an extremely silly thing to wear, too, which is why you'll see relatively roomy shirts onstage.

Every single percentage point of advantage counts at the top level; shirts may look like a psychedelic nightmare but you can bet that the players have chosen them ultimately for comfort. What's printed on them sends a message to opponents, looks great on TV and satisfies the sponsors, sure, but if it feels crappy, the player's going to have a mare when it's game on – style eventually has to come second to substance. If it stops you throwing, it's gotta get chucked pretty sharpish, even if it does look badass in the mirror.

QUIZ

THE HISTORY OF DARTS

Let's dive into the history of the greatest sport on the planet – kabaddi. What? Oh, right. Darts. The double toppermost of the poppermost, the game of skill and psychology, the only sport in the world in which you have to hold your breath and invade your opponents' court while also repeating the word 'kabaddi' . . . no, hang on, that's not right either. No more messing about, let's have a quiz all about the history of our wonderful game. As they say: Let's! Play! Kabaddi! We mean darts!

1. Who (probably) invented darts?

a. St Darts, the patron saint of lobbing spiky things at trees
b. Medieval soldiers, circa 1300, chucking short arrows/spearheads at wine barrels
c. Bobby George, after his modelling career went west

2. The modern game of darts most likely originates where?

a. France, 19th century, using metal-pointed wooden *fléchettes* with turkey-feather flights
b. Holland, 18th century, using discarded dyke spikes with papier-mâché flights
c. England, 20th century, using tungsten-tipped darts made by Winmau, previously a drinks company

3. At which travelling show would you be most likely to encounter early dartboards and darts?

a. Circus
b. Fairground
c. Theatre

4. According to lore, in 1511 a tavern boss called William Bray invented what?

a. A dartboard
b. A dart sharpener
c. Happy hour

5. Which king of England was an avid darts player? (Clue: his second wife gifted him a set of special darts to play with.)

a. Henry V
b. Edward the Confessor
c. Henry VIII

6. It is said that in 1896 a certain Lancastrian carpenter standardised the numbering system that we now see on a modern competition dartboard. Do you know his name?

a. Brian Gamlin
b. Dave Barnett
c. Michael Johnston

7. In what year did Jim Garside, landlord of the Adelphi Inn in Leeds, go to court in order to have darts declared a game of skill – and therefore eligible to be played in public houses?

a. 1822
b. 1722
c. 1908

8. How did that landlord go about proving it was, indeed, a skilled game?

a. He invited the judge to come down to the pub and take on all-comers
b. He brought in the region's best player, William 'Bigfoot' Anakin, who hit a 180 in court
c. He brought in 16 of the region's best players and they played a knockout tournament in court

9. In what year was the National Darts Association formed, in order to standardise rules?

a. 1980
b. 1880
c. 1925

10. In 1935, a chemist called Ted Leggatt teamed up with Frank Dabbs to do what?

a. Use bundles of sisal to create more durable dartboards than the wooden ones
b. Use metal to strengthen the barrels of previously wooden darts
c. Create the world's first kabaddi league

11. What was unusual about the 'sports packs' issued to soldiers in the Second World War?

a. They had a set of darts included
b. They had a dartboard included
c. They had a dart scoring chart included

12. In which year was the World Darts Federation formed?

a. 1972
b. 1974
c. 1988

13. What was the first broadcast date for darts on British television?

a. 1936
b. 1972
c. 1944

14. The *News of the World* Championship once ruled the roost. In which year did people first enjoy it on telly?

a. 1936
b. 1972
c. 1944

15. And do you know which year the first *News of the World* Championship took place?

a. 1936
b. 1927
c. 1944

16. Which innovation did a BBC producer called Nick Hunter introduce?

a. Walk-on music
b. Microphones onstage
c. Split screen for TV

17. Which seismic event happened in 1993?

a. Eric Bristow lost for the first time to Phil Taylor
b. Disgruntled players split from the BDO to run their own darts competitions
c. The BBC decided to show darts 24/7 on a special red button channel

18. A famous 1980 comedy sketch featuring Griff Rhys Jones and Mel Smith featured two players doing what instead of throwing darts?

a. Having a sumo wrestling fight
b. Throwing frisbees over a fence
c. Having various alcoholic drinks

19. Fallon Sherrock did what in 2019?

a. Became the first female professional
b. Became the first woman to win a PDC World Championship match
c. Became a sponsor for the European Championships of kabaddi

20. How old was Luke Littler when he became PDC World Champion?

a. 16
b. 19
c. 17

'Big Cliff Lazarenko's idea of exercise is sitting in a room with the windows open, taking the lid off something cool and fizzy.'

'This is super-calla-non-fragile-ballistics.'

QUIZ

ANATOMY OF A DART

You can't play without 'em – simple as that. Hold 'em by the non-pointy bit and chuck them towards the round thing so the pointy end sticks in the round thing roughly where you aimed it. Simple when you know how, isn't it? But how much do you know about the key equipment itself – the dart? All questions here are according to the *DRA Rule Book*, so quarrel with them if you disagree. Some tricky soft-tip ones here, too!

1. What are the four standard sections of a dart?

a. Point, barrel, flight, stem

b. Point, top, bottom, wings

c. Point, barrel, speed, stick

2. What is the maximum length for a dart?

a. 500mm

b. 200mm

c. There is no maximum

3. And the maximum weight?

a. 100 grams

b. 1 tonne

c. 40 grams

4. What the living heck is the significance of these three rules? A point for each.

a. Your dart point, within 15mm of the point, is coarser than #18 on a VDI 3400 gauge

b. Your tip has a ridge, a groove or anything else like that on the surface within 15mm of the point – unless it is in general parallel to the tip's length

c. Your tip's diameter or cross section, within that 15mm length of the end again, is more than 2.5 mm

5. What is the likely consequence of having very blunt or flat darts?

a. Bounce-outs
b. Scraped hands
c. They won't fly

6. What is the restriction on the dart-throwing action?

a. There are no restrictions – go for it!
b. Underarm is allowed only once a year
c. Overarm only

7. What are metal tips usually made of, when using a common (bristle) dartboard?

a. Tungsten, nickel and steel alloys
b. Graphite, carbon and stainless steel alloys
c. Dilithium crystals, Captain's Logs and Worf spit

8. Describe a 'moveable point dart'. *(No clues this time – soz!)*

9. What is a soft-tip dart, and when would it be used?

a. With a non-metal tip (usually plastic), for special boards

b. Disposable tips, changed every game

c. Special metal, only for championships

10. What is the name of the World Championship of Soft-Tipped Darts?

a. The World

b. Hard Play, Soft Tips

c. Universal Darts

11. And which organisation is behind it?

a. Bristow's Greatest Dartists

b. DARTSLIVE

c. World Darts Group

12. Which televised nine-darter superstar is a multiple soft-tip champion?

a. Luke Littler

b. John Lowe

c. Paul Lim

13. Which Croatian professional steel-tip PDC player absolutely bossed soft-tip events, starting in around 2005?

a. Bojan 'Bam Bam' Djokovic
b. Goran 'Boof Boof' Krampus
c. Boris 'Dum Dum' Krčmar

14. Back to steel-tip rules now: how many different darts can a player use in any one match?

a. Only their stated three
b. Any amount
c. Six, but they must be identical

15. Under which circumstances can a dropped dart be used during a turn?

a. If you, the opponent and the ref all agree
b. If it is dropped before your throwing action
c. If it has not travelled more than three feet

16. What happens if, after you've hit Game Shot, you continue to throw?

a. You will bust
b. Nothing
c. Your opponent wins

17. In which three circumstances can throwing fewer than three darts signify the end of your visit?

a. If your opponent calls a foul throw; if the referee deems it too noisy; if you have thrown too many darts in that leg already

b. If you've agreed that the highest score wins; if your opponent calls a timeout; if you call a timeout

c. If you touch a dart that's already sticking in the dartboard during your visit; if you hit a winner (i.e. a finish double); if you bust your score before three darts have been thrown ('no score' will be called)

18. Paradoxically, a player who regularly can throw very tightly grouped darts will find their accuracy technically decreases – why might that be?

a. Tiny nicks will affect aerodynamic performance

b. They'll get complacent and start to miss

c. The darts will get hot and friction increases

19. There is a third kind of tipped dart and generally these are fun ones for youngsters. What are they?

a. Compostable tips

b. Magnetic tips

c. Plasticine tips

20. Let's go outside – yes, that's the rainy place where there's generally no bar and it's cold – and, hey! There's some people chucking massive things that look remarkably like actual darts! What game are they likely to be playing?

a. Hide the sausage

b. Darts for dinglers

c. Lawn darts

DARTS LEGEND

Name: Eric Bristow, MBE (awarded 1989)

Nickname: The Crafty Cockney

Date of birth: 25th April, 1957

Place of birth: Hackney, London

Died: 5th April, 2018 (age 60)

Active since: Took up the game age 11, left school at 14, first title (World Masters) 1977

Darts: 22g 'Eric Bristow' Harrows

Walk-On Music: Chas & Dave: 'Rabbit'

Shirt: Usually featured a police officer, the Union Jack flag and his nickname (originally taken from a pub named the same in Santa Monica, California, around 1976).

Notable Achievements: Five world championships, five world Masters, *News of the World* double champion, three British Matchplays, and many, many other wins across the world of darts. Mentored Phil 'The Power' Taylor, lending him a significant sum to enable Taylor to go full-time at darts. Had an instantly recognisable style in which his little finger would stick out at a right angle. Presented *Bullseye* for the very first two/pilot episodes! Look at what we could have won . . .

Controversies: Oof, where to begin . . .? Allegedly kept a claw hammer on his person as a young man about town, and that his gang, the Oxton Boys, broke into houses to burgle them; said that when he worked in a suit factory he would wear baggy clothes on Fridays, under which he'd hide a suit and take it home; smoked 40 a day; slept with countless women on tour; suffered from dartitis for a decade; appeared in typically unrepentant style on *Celebrity Big Brother* (2012); accused of spousal assault (then cleared) in 2005; sacked by Sky Sports after posting a series of tweets about football's sexual abuse scandal, in which he wrote that darts players were 'tough guys' while footballers were 'wimps' – and later apologised, calling himself a 'bull in a china shop' whose wording had been incorrect and offended 'many people'; BBC later reported his management had asked for a fee of £5,000 in order to appear on air to talk about the issue. The BBC declined, but Bristow said 'any monies offered or received for any interviews with me will be donated in full to a relevant charity'; a confirmed pet lover with at one stage a household clowder of 11 cats – his partner in his latter years worked for a rehoming charity.

Quote: 'You can trust an animal. An animal doesn't stab you in the back.'

> **'This is a very, very grey patch from Taylor. The sort of patch you see on a tramp's pants.'**

STAND AND DELIVER

How to throw darts . . . it's got a lot more moving parts than you might think, folks.

It's a simple game, but to master anything in life requires consistency and technique. There are a few things to consider when we're stepping up to the oche, and not all of them are obvious.

First off, how do you actually stand? Where do you put your feet when you're ready to throw? The stance is one of the most fundamental skills in the sport. You might say it's something that should come naturally – and yet second-guessing yourself can lead to all sorts of problems with balance. Bad balance is an absolute guarantee of bad aim, and bad aim is the road towards losing darts matches as well as getting ripely peeved at the whole darn kaboodle.

There are countless variations on stances but we can distil them to three main ones. First off, it's the good old open stance, where you face the board standing more or less normally, weight equally distributed between both feet, which touch the oche at their toes. You might hear this one also called a front stance, for obvious reasons.

It gives you the best stereographic image as your eyes are both on the same visual locus, and throwing from directly over your nose should give your dart the best chance of going where you're looking.

You'll probably see most professionals use closed stance. This is best thought of as a side-on stance; that is, your body is angled about 90 degrees from the board. If you are a right-handed thrower, your right foot will be up against the oche and vice versa for lefties. As you can immediately feel with this one, your weight is now on the front foot, closer to the board, and your back foot serves mostly as balance rather than ballast. In terms of vision, you're now getting used to the depth perception difference between the right and left eyes, which are now at different distances to the board.

Halfway between open and closed is forwards stance, where you are standing at about 20 degrees from the oche, your dominant foot forwards. It's a way to work towards the closed stance while retaining more visual depth than with closed. Generally, if you look at kids playing darts, they'll be either open stance or forwards at best, unless they're another little Littler in the making, of course.

Grip this

But how do you hold a dart? Well, that comes naturally, too. Bristow's little-finger-out grip was unusual but worked for him; the most important thing is that the dart weight feels good in your hand and that the balance is correct. But whether you use two, three or four fingers, or hold the dart close to, or away from, the flights, stability is the absolute key. You need to be holding it steady, but for the love of Zeus do not squeeze the dart too tight. If you feel like the dart's gasping for breath, something's wrong. If it's wobbling all over the shop, then you need to adjust your grip strength and placement on the barrel. Practise, practise, practise.

Hints:

- Keep your shoulder, elbow, hand and eye straight and aligned with each other.
- Look at the board rather than the dart.
- You might initially want to close your non-dominant eye (i.e. left eye for righties) to help aim.
- Watch those elbows: they may move up or down when you chuck and that will mean darts go badly off course.
- Throw the dart. You don't need to launch it as

hard as possible – go for a nice, confident arc that feels good. It shouldn't hurt to throw! If it does, something's out of whack, or you may have an injury that needs looking at.

- Keep your feet on the floor – that balancing back foot must not wobble as it will send darts off course, which does not take much at all.
- Practise from different parts of the oche – change the angle. You'll see players do this when they're trying to sneak a third dart into a full-looking treble bed, or perhaps they've had two near-misses at a double and need to find a way to avoid hitting their previous darts. It will stand you in great stead to be comfortable with changing the angle (and training your eyes to get used to different views of the board).
- Vary the speed at which you take your three throws. If you're usually a thinker who takes your sweet time to aim and then languidly sends the dart towards the board, speed up and see what happens when you rely on your instincts instead. If you're a swift thrower, take a breath before you'd normally throw and be a little more deliberate. Variation can help you if your

opponent's a very fast player – you can keep up with them, or equally you can slow your game down to hopefully make them slow down and not play their natural game. Psychology is everywhere in this wonderful sport!

- Relax. Yep, the most annoying advice anyone can give to any other person who's in an excited state – take it easy. But it's true. Tension in the brain transfers to the muscles all too easily as we see constantly when the pressure is on even the greatest players. Emotions are never far from the surface and nobody's asking you to be a robot, but if you can control your heart rate when the chips are down, your chances of winning tight games just increased. There's always plenty of time to let out that emotion after the game or on the winning shots. But remember, once you've had those three darts then that visit's gone. Once you've done a nine-darter, it's just one leg in a match. Once someone's stolen a close game against the darts and you've missed seven chances at a double, that's done and dusted. Clear your mind, relax and start again from 501. Good luck, champ!

PLAY IT: NOUGHTS AND CROSSES (ALSO KNOWN AS: TIC-TAC-TOE, X AND O)

GAME

Players:

Two, or two teams

In brief:

Hit the right targets to create three Xs or Os in a row.

How to play:

Player/team one is X and player two is O. First draw the traditional noughts and crosses grid on the scoreboard. So far, so simple. Setting up the active scoring numbers requires visualising that grid on top of a traditional dartboard. So, the centre of our notional 3x3 grid is the bull – think of this as the middle square. The left-hand square of the middle row, then, is 11, and the right-hand square of the middle is 6, with bull the centre. Let's now do the middle column: 20 and 3, with the bull at centre too. Now we have a cross, so it's time to fill in the corners of our grid. The top left-hand corner is 12, the top-right 18; the bottom-left is 8 and bottom-right 7. The grid looks like this:

12 – 20 – 18
11– bull – 6
8 – 3 – 7

These are the only active targets. Doubles and trebles are treated as singles here as there's no additive scoring: merely the chase towards three in a row either horizontally, vertically or diagonally.

Work out who will throw first by any method you choose: longest middle toe or something like that.

To make this as exciting as possible this is a one-dart-per-turn game, that is, player/team one throws to secure a number, e.g. bull. Draw an X in the middle of the scoreboard grid. Nobody can cancel the X. Player/team two then throws to start off their own quest for three-in-a-row and hits, say, 20. That blocks off the 20–bull–3 three-in-a-row possibility for X, and opens up 12–20–18 for O. Keep going until someone has secured three in a row. In a team game, the next player of team one throws, and so on.

As with the on-paper game, it's now down to tactics – or tic-tac-toes – and trying to lure your opponent into leaving you a mistake. In our example game, player one would possibly block off O by getting 12, which also opens up the potential 12–bull–7 diagonal to win. Player two would probably go for 7 to block. If they missed, then player one has a shot at 7 to win . . .

The difference in this darts version is that you don't need to throw to block, if you're confident that you/ your team is more skilful. It's possible player one aims at 12 and misses, in which case player two is absolutely within their rights to go for that number and set up 12–20–18. Player one might then choose to hit 11, setting up 11–bull–6 but banking on a miss by player two. Do you dare to be so bold? Noughts and crosses ain't a game for the faint-hearted . . .

Variation one

Three darts each. This of course means you might win on your first visit. Well, so be it: clear the scoreboard and let player two try to do the same. First to 10 games wins. Once the grid is agreed then you can pretty much go wherever you like with it.

Variation two

Use only doubles or treble beds, plus inner bull to make it super-tough.

Variation three

Killer crosses. In this game you *can* cancel the other person's numbers, so if player one hits bull, you can open it up again by hitting the bull as player two.

Variation four

Three darts to close up. A number only scores once either player has hit it three times; doubles and trebles are in play on this one. You can cancel their darts as per variation three, but once a player has secured three scores on their target number, it goes down as an X or O on the scoreboard and cannot be cancelled.

'He's been burning the midnight oil at both ends.'

BROS: WHEN WILL I BE FAMOUS (FOR PLAYING DARTS)?

In the midst of the neon-weirdness of the 1980s, one pop band reigned supreme. They were a trio, with a set of twins – Matt and Luke Goss – plus their mate Craig Logan (later rechristened 'Ken' by the mighty *Viz*). Due to the twins factor they were named Bros, and teenage girls dampened their kecks as they squealed their love to the blond-haired duo (Craig, poor lad, was a distant third).

Bros were huge stars for about four years before – as is the way of things in pop music – their time at number one was firmly over, and they split up. Lead singer Matt was the most successful, going on to have several chart hits plus residencies at various clubs in Las Vegas.

In 2017 the brothers got back together for some celebrated reunion gigs (Logan declined to be involved) and a very entertaining documentary called *Bros: After the Screaming Stops* was released the following year.

Among the family arguments and occasionally fractious rehearsals, the boys also revisited their childhood home, outside of which Matt revealed one of their favourite toys as kids.

A dart.

Not a set of darts, nor a dartboard, but a single, solitary dart.

'We used to throw it up in the air as hard as we could,' said Matt. The boys would then stay as still as possible and wait for it to land again. Inevitably, one time the dart did actually hit him, piercing the skin near his rib. His grandad pulled it out and, undaunted, the boys started the game again immediately. Heroes all.

Matt went on to rather dilute the anecdote by straight away going on a bizarre rant about how people weren't allowed to play conkers in England anymore, which kind of sums up the roller-coaster nature of the documentary.

We're not sure we'll see the 'Chucking Darts Up and Standing Still' championships at the Lakeside any time soon, to be honest.

'He's about as predictable as a wasp on speed.'

GETTING ON THE TOUR (Q-SCHOOL)

We love the darts, which is why we're standing up while we write this. We love watching the competitive nature of the various championships, including league games when we're pulling a sickie from work/definitely ill *cough, splutter*. We also love a good hard-fought game of our own. But have you ever imagined what it'd be like to actually mix it with the pros? Well, there's no need to sit down and play the 'what if' game when you can try to qualify for the actual tour. Welcome, folks, to Q-School.

PDC Qualifying Schools, to give them their full name, began after the 2011 World Championship. The prize on offer is a two-year tour card that allows entry to professional-level tournaments. The Q-Schools are available and open to any of us as long as we're aged 16 or over, whether an amateur player or indeed a former pro who has lost their tour card – that means they've dropped out of the top 64 in the rankings, which in turn means they're going to be pretty darned sharp players, so it's tough, tough, tough.

Q-Schools take place each January in various venues: for British-based players (including Northern Ireland and Gibraltar), that's Milton Keynes, and for European dartists, it's Niedernhausen, Germany. Non-European contenders can decide whether to compete in Germany or Milton Keynes. Should you last the distance, the entire qualifying stages last seven days in total, with all games being best of 11 legs.

There's a three-day first stage with up to 128 hopefuls per venue, and eight quarter-finalists per day are taken through to the final stage from this preliminary round – day winners of each first stage competition automatically get a tour card.

The remaining places in the final stage are taken from the Order of Merit. Each win during the tournament gives you a point, so once the day's qualifiers have gone through, the better players on the list then go on to fill in the rest of the schedule. But there's a little more to it!

Those who've dropped off the tour and thus lost their card the previous season are exempt from the prelims so join at the final stage, though they must still enter the Q-School along with everyone else. The top 16 from the Winmau Challenge Tour and Development Tour Order of Merit also go straight through to the finals.

As well as this the top eight from the Women's Series Order of Merit, and the PDC Nordic and Baltic Tour are given free entry to the first stage of the school. The PDC also has the right to extend invitations to nominated players – John Part, for example.

At stake during the final stage are up to 32 tour cards, which give access to the pro tour – some 30 Players' Championships, and 13 or so European Tour events per year. You can also enter qualifying events for the biggies like the World, European, Matchplay and Grand Slam events with a tour card. It also assists you because you are able to play in ranking events that solidify your position in that all-important top 64 (UK/Europe). Playing in Q-School regardless allows you to join the Challenge Tour, which, as noted above, can get you through to the next year's final stage if you're successful.

It may seem Byzantine and complex but the basic FAQ is simple:

- Anyone can apply to join Qualifying School (it costs a few hundred quid, so check the PDC site).
- The best players at Q-School go through with averages of 85 upwards, in 16-dart legs or thereabouts.

So, get practising, and practising hard, way before you even attempt to mix it with the folks at Q-School. Think of it more like the final step towards a whole new world rather than a chance to assess how good you actually are. Yes, you'll get some people at the schools knocking out averages of 40–50, but there's a snowball's chance in hell of them ever getting near to the final stage, let alone the promised land of a tour card.

All that said, the tour does have a constant need to renew itself, whether that be from players retiring or new blood replacing out-of-form old stagers. There are caveats as detailed herewith but generally it's a system designed to bring in the very best new talent. If you're good enough, then you'll get yourself through the stages while also experiencing some of the pressure and match-day nerves of the big kahunas. If it doesn't work out? Well, there's always next year, or the year after that . . .

'Darts players are probably a lot fitter than most footballers in overall body strength.'

'He's too fast for his own good. It's like an octopus with toothache; you start thinking about your mouth instead of your feet. Too many moving parts.'

QUIZ

WHO SAID IT?

Like any one-on-one sport, darts has a huge psychological side: when each player is equally matched, more often than not the difference between winning and losing comes down to temperament. Players also come from all sorts of backgrounds, both geographically and demographically. This can make for some excellent utterances from the heroes of the sport, whether in the heat of battle, analysing darts as a whole or reminiscing about how they got started in the game.

We've put a bunch of quotes together – your job is simply to match them to the player who said them.

We've fiendishly put the wrong player's name to the quotes below to confuse matters even more. How will you get on?

'I am on a fat-free diet for most of the year, but before the Worlds I tend to relax on the diet a bit to concentrate on darts.' – **Adrian Lewis**

'I'd missed the boat in rugby, I was stuck in a rut and I needed a change. I was lucky to have darts as an option.' – **Michael van Gerwen**

'All this cuddling and kissing on stage these days, well it's all right in football when someone scores a goal, but not when you're playing darts.' – **Fallon Sherrock**

'I always wear flat shoes for darts because a heel can put me off balance.' – **Bobby George**

'I've beaten two of the best players in the world, and if that doesn't say that women can't play darts, I don't know what can.' – **John Part**

'I can offer my family things that I could never have dreamed of – darts has changed my life.'
– **Gerwyn Price**

'I got into darts from watching it on TV, and I used to joke with my friends: "I could do that, I could be the best in the world." I told them I'd be the world champion.' – **Luke Littler**

'If I look at the standard of darts on TV, I think I have taken it to a new level.' – **Rob Cross**

'I don't have any GCSEs, everyone probably has more than me. Although I did pass my sport.' – **Eric Bristow**

'Lucky I'm an old man now. When I was younger, I would have won the handsome stakes hands down.'
– **Phil Taylor**

PLAY IT: ROUND THE BOARD

GAME

Also known as:

Round the world; around the clock; once around the island

Players:

From one to everyone

In brief:

Get around the board as quickly as you can by hitting each number from 1 upwards and ending on the bull.

How to play:

Take it in turns, three darts each. Start at 1. First to hit the bull wins. The only darts that matter are the ones that hit the bed you are aiming for: you can't bank, say, a treble 20 for future use. Nope, if you're aiming for the number 1 then only darts that hit the number 1 count. Move on as soon as you've hit the number you require.

A note about the bull: the inner bull is technically a double 25. You can choose to upgrade that to a notional treble – in which case, you could decide that it's acceptable to hit three outer bulls to check out rather than a single inner.

Variation one: leapfrog

Hit the double and you leapfrog one number. So, if you are on 1 and hit double 1, you don't have to hit the 2, and move straight on to 3. Hit a treble and leapfrog two numbers, e.g. if you are on 3 and hit treble 3, you will miss 4 and 5 and therefore move straight to 6. These rules do not apply to 20 or the bull. So, for example, if you hit a treble 19, you can only move on to the bull (miss out 20), and a treble 20 has no further effect – you still need to hit a bull.

You can choose to finish on a double bull or not – but make sure everyone knows at the start of the game!

Variation two: double trouble

Same as the basic game but go around the board *only* hitting doubles. Singles and trebles do not count (aside from double bull, as above).

Variation three: treble in paradise

Same as double trouble but only treble beds are active, aside from double bull.

> Variations two and three are also good ways to level up standards – if you're playing against the local pro then they have to hit only doubles or trebles while the rest of the players are free to pick off the singles. The better players should welcome this and treat it as an excellent practice opportunity.

Variation four: winner stays on

If a player hits three active targets in one visit then they retrieve their darts for another visit. This continues until they miss. And, yes, it can be incredibly annoying if someone's extremely good at darts 'cause theoretically if they go first then they can win without anyone else having a visit at all. *C'est la vie*, folks.

Variation five: three darts, one score

Each player must hit a single, double and treble of each number (leaving out the bull on this one) – and add up their own points (i.e. the actual score achieved on the active number only) as they go. You probably want to use the scoreboard for this one. Highest score wins.

Variation on the variation

You only get one visit per number to achieve this. This means the scoring is even more important.

Award one point for a single, two for a double and three for a treble regardless of the actual numbers on the board (i.e. if you are on 9s then hitting single (1), double (2) and treble (3) is six points).

Variation two on the variation

You must score three to continue. That is, hit a treble, a double and a single, or three singles before you can move forwards. Note that this also forms the basis of another game, Shanghai, elsewhere in this book.

Variation six: flip reverse it

Start at 20 and work your way down to 1. You can either begin with a double bull or end with one, by prior arrangement.

THE GREAT SPLIT: WHAT HAPPENED IN 1993?

Over 30 years ago a huge schism happened in darts, changing the professional game forever. But what was it all about?

To explain it, we have to go back a few years – the 1970s saw a huge explosion in interest in the game, moving into the dominant early 1980s in which the likes of John Lowe, Jocky Wilson and Eric Bristow were massive household names. You'd see the championships on telly, and on the weekend there was also *Bullseye*, the iconic Jim Bowen-presented quiz-and-chuck game that had families glued to their tellies. Warning: many initialisms follow.

At that time the British Darts Organisation was in charge, from the grass roots all the way up to the World Championship (which first took place in 1978). The BDO had in 1973 taken over from the venerable National Darts Association of Great Britain (established 1954). The NDAGB was a new set-up based on the previous National Darts Association, which had been established in 1925 to standardise rules. The BDO breathed new life into the sport – some eight million watched John Lowe defeat Leighton Rees in the 1979 Embassy World Professional Darts Championship final. Note that the sponsors were cigarette manufacturers – a relic of a different era for sure.

The same people behind the BDO, including the influential Olly Croft, also established the World Darts Federation back in 1976. The intent was to promote the game worldwide, widening participation outside of the shores of the UK.

As to world championships, well, there were technically two of them running at the same time in those days. The *News of the World* Championship had been running since the 1940s, originally as a UK event, but faded from view during the 1980s – even as the BDO Worlds was rising. Sponsors were hard to get, there was no prize money and it finally went to the wall in 1990 (with a one-year revival in 1996–97, won by Phil Taylor).

TV coverage was also being cut back during the 1980s; *World of Sport*, which had featured darts heavily, was cancelled on ITV in 1985, and the Winmau World Masters was covered also by that channel until 1988. By that year, all the BBC was showing was the Embassy World Professional Darts Championship. By the end of the eighties, then, the ubiquity of darts was over and the sport's time on telly was massively restricted. For pro darts players, this meant a huge downturn in prize money, and without day jobs to fall back on, it directly affected their ability to continue to compete at all. Something had to be done.

Rebel rebel

It was player power that led the rebellion; 16 of the top players in the world got together to found a new governing body, the World Darts Council, in January 1992. The likes of Lowe, Dennis Priestley, Keith Deller, Taylor and Eric Bristow were involved – recognisable, bankable names, in other words – and 18 months later, the WDC's first event was televised by Anglia TV.

At the 1993 BDO World Championships, the rebel players intended to wear WDC badges to show their disapproval of how things were run; in the event, they did not do so but the die was cast (John Lowe became champion of essentially the final unified darts championship). Following the Worlds, the top players gathered at the Rose and Thistle public house in Frimley to tell reporters that they intended to boycott the next BDO worlds if Olly Croft did not recognise the nascent

WDC. However, rather than integrate the WDC's ideas to the existing governing bodies, both the BDO and the WDF banned all those players from any events – including at a county level.

Enter Sky Sports, a new player in the broadcast field and hoovering up sports to fill their new 24-hour channel. Sky would cover a WDF World Championship that began on Boxing Day 1993, running to 2nd January, 1994, and sponsored by Skol lager. The timing was not coincidental – it was immediately before the traditional start of the BDO World Championships. Provocative, yes. Star-studded – you betcha. Fourteen of the 16 original rebels would compete as Chris Johns and Mike Gregory had decided to return to the BDO; they would be replaced by Kevin Burrows and Graeme Stoddart, defying the BDO in turn; seven US entrants and one Irishman finalised the field. The inaugural WDC Worlds were won in style by Priestley, who hammered Phil Taylor 6–1 and in so doing became the first to win both the BDO and WDC championships.

As for the BDO's tournament, well, it was shorn of most of the current superstars but still boasted the likes of Bobby George and eventual winner, Canadian star John Part. Part retained his title the following year.

Court cases were rampaging, with lost earnings and restraint of trade being cited by the WDC players against the BDO, who they saw as a monopoly. They also argued that their ban was in violation of the law of the European Union. It ran on and on, with legal fees rising, and on 30th June, 1997, the judge ruled that the WDC players had indeed been restricted unreasonably. The BDO's worldwide ban was lifted, and the WDC events recognised. The WDC also dropped all damages claims for loss of earnings, agreeing as well to rebrand as the Professional Darts Corporation. This removed 'world' from their name; the PDC recognised that the WDF was the worldwide governing body and the BDO the governing body in the UK.

How it stands today

There were various permutations of which championships players could enter (or not) during the 1990s and 2000s, before we reached today's situation whereby all PDC majors can only be entered by members of the Professional Dart Players Association. Holding a PDC tour card is essential and every year qualifying school competitions take place to refresh the ranks. There are exceptions: if you are resident in the host country of a

PDPA Players or Open event, you can take part. For the televised contests in the Netherlands under BDO rules, they are allowed to invite a certain amount of PDC 'wild card' entrants (this was largely so Raymond van Barneveld could compete in the 2000s). Grand Slam of Darts events can also include both BDO and PDC players, televised by ITV.

As well as Sky TV, a key player got involved in 2001: Barry Hearn. Installed as chairman, he got to work to establish the PDC Pro Tour and under his management the prize money increased considerably, with prize pots now easily totalling in the millions. This was more than enough to attract the stragglers from the BDO, including Barney, who was keen to pit his skills against the likes of The Power. As a result, the BDO has begun to appear more like a feeder tour to the PDC. Indeed, in 2009, Hearn offered to buy the BDO out entirely. The takeover bid was eventually rejected despite pressure from county organisations.

By 2018, the BDO itself had a new chairman in Des Jacklin, and as of 1st October that year, all PDC tour carders would be allowed into all BDO events, while all BDO-affiliated darts players were now able to enter Q-School without sanctions. The PDC is at this point far ahead of its BDO counterpart in terms of prize money, arguably player quality and profile; while BDO and WDF events still form an important part of the darts calendar, it's surely only a matter of time before the British Darts Organisation is somehow folded into the PDC. The last thing anybody wants is a repeat of the farce in boxing, where there can be up to four 'world champions' at the same time.

It'll also make it easier to read about darts without all these blimmin' initialisms, too. Let's hope for peace in our time, and averages of 110+ while we're at it.

'The atmosphere is so tense, if Elvis walked in with a portion of chips, you could hear the vinegar sizzle on them.'

CALCULATING YOUR FINISH

It's all about the maths when it comes down to crunch time. Every player needs to know how to calculate a finish with three darts – getting this wrong and missing a checkout opportunity is an absolute no-no and will cost you more games than missing your trebles. But is there a simple way to work out how to end on a double?

The short answer to that is 'no', unfortunately, but there are some steps you can take to ensure that you're efficient with your set-ups.

When we're learning, the temptation is to take the potential finish, say 138, and count down from there. So, let's say 138 – 60 = 78. So T20 is the first shot. That leaves us 78. If we want to try and finish on double top that means we need to take away 38. That's D19, so the outshot is T20, D19, D20. Not the easiest. You see the problem? We always want to finish on a double but not have to use a double to get there.

An alternative you're more likely to see is the Deller checkout: T20, T18, D12. There are numerous other ways to achieve this, including the equally popular T19, 19, D12, which is excellent for close-groupers, or one used sometimes by Adrian Lewis and a bit risky: T20, T20, D9. Why risky? Well, with the D12 checkouts, hitting a single means leaving another double – D6 – whereas hitting a single 9 would mean you'd need two darts to subsequently get to the double (3 D3 or, more likely, 5 D2). As a rule, you want to be able to leave a double every time if you hit the single instead – hence why 32 is always a target.

You can get darts checkout charts – hang one of these next to the board and refer to it every time you're on a finish. This will help solidify the most popular checkouts in your game. Indeed, you can work your way down from 170 here and if you miss the big 'un, you'll be able to instantly see what you've left. Similarly, any electronic dartboard/set-up should have a function for showing you a possible out, and there's loads of apps so you can refer to them too. But there's nothing like having them in your own head – so here are some hints.

Some tips

First off – and this may sound basic, but it's a golden rule – it's absolutely essential to know your doubles. Double top is not 20 + 20, then, but always 40. The double segment of 16 is always 32. The double segment of 6 is always 12. It's a slightly different way of looking at the dartboard, but as you learn each segment's value and location on the board it will eventually become second nature. Indeed, there's nothing stopping you from marking the doubles on your home practice board with their *actual* values. Use correction fluid or a silver/gold pen and if you don't mind your board looking scruffy, it's gonna help a huge amount. Think of it in a similar way to learning to play the guitar or piano: if you mark the frets/notes, you'll have a massive advantage in learning your scales. Same applies here.

Try this: a game using doubles only. You can either go down from 501 or simply decide to take nine darts and see how high your score can be. The catch? You can only count in doubles. So, as above, a D19 is always 38 and that's the only number you can mention. A session of round the board with doubles only is also a great exercise.

It's all about the previous visit

In fact, what we're really looking for is a four- or five-dart finish, in other words setting up a decent last three darts on the previous visit. If you think about it, it makes complete sense: the first visit is all about piling on the points – going for the maximum – and the second probably will be too, unless you're on for a nine-darter. For mere mortals, though, dart six and onwards are geared towards the finish line.

Say, after five darts, you've scored 140 on first visit and a further 120 so far on visit two, a total of 260 and leaving 241 (awesome play, by the way, this is looking at a 100+ average). How do we get to a double from here? Moving towards the winning post in the fewest darts is a psychological fillip for you and a real challenge towards your opponent. As there's no four-dart finish available, you're still looking to pile the points on: another 60 leaves 181, not a finish. Being canny, you might switch down under and go for T19 or even T17 to knock off that odd number. Using the latter, you're then on 190; how you use the four darts (two visits) from there is up to you. That means on the next visit you can set up a single shot at a double for your tenth dart – and indeed three shots at it – by working out your best checkout.

Sometimes, your opponent will be looking at a finish before you, in which case a heavy score with your next visit that also sets up a single-dart double for the visit after that is really going to put the pressure on them.

Checkout cards

You can make these yourself – simply write every number starting at 41 and ending at 170 on different postcards/ pieces of paper. Pick them out of a hat without looking. Whichever number you get, you must finish in three darts (or fewer). You'll find there are countless ways to get to many of the finishes. Try to hit each checkout, no matter how many darts it takes you. A version of this is catch 40, where you have six darts only at each score (generally between 61 and 100). Practising this will fix some of these in your head.

The two-dart rule of threes

If you've got 65 left, taking away T20 = 5. Not a finish. So, take away 3 from 60 = 57 = T19 and add it to 5 = 8. So, you have a finish of T19, D4. Not bad! This way isn't perfect, but it's a shortcut to remember. Let's do a couple more: 77. So: 77 – 60 = 17 – not an out. Take away 3 from 60: 77 – 57 = 20. So, the out is T19, D10. So: 83 – 60 = 23 – not a double. But 83 – 57 = 26. Outshot then is T19, D13. In order to get to a better double, keep adding and taking away the three. We want D16 ideally as an outshot, so let's go back to the original calculation. As 83 – 60 = 23, we need to add 9 to that final number (23) in order to get to D16 (32). So, we must also remember to take that away from the original (T20): 60 – 9 = 51, leaving us with what we all know is a slinky T17. The outshot here for 83, and much more darts-friendly, is therefore T17 – D16. Cool, huh?

Whichever way you practise, it's all down to learning your outshots – and in the process learning your game. You'll notice different players will favour different outshots. The only reason for that is that they prefer certain ways to finish. Indeed, the only 'right' way to finish is the one that ends with the call of 'Game shot!' as you see your dart land beautifully in the centre of that doubles bed. Or, hanging on somehow by its very tip and just inside the double – they all count, even if you can't.

A word about bogeys

These are scores under 180 that can't be finished with three darts on a double. The only thing to do is to learn 'em, folks: 169, 168, 166, 165, 163, 162 and 159. Leaving yourself with three darts at any of these is a horrendous error and means you need to buy everyone in the venue a pint. Well, it oughta anyway. As you can see, this is one of the chief reasons that you need to think about the finish several darts before you get to the single-visit nitty-gritty. With a single dart left in hand, you'll want to avoid setting any of these little buggers up for your next visit, so just take a pause if you're at that stage and do some quick calculations between your current score and the ones you want to avoid at all costs.

'William Tell could take an apple off your head, [Phil] Taylor could take out a processed pea.'

'When Alexander of Macedonia was 33, he cried salt tears because there were no more worlds to conquer. Bristow's only 27.'

'If we'd had Phil Taylor at Hastings against the Normans, they'd have gone home.'

CAN YOU HIT THE BULLSEYE?

Frank Sinatra claimed to be the 'Chairman of the Board'. Years later, Iggy Pop told us he was the 'Chairman of the Bored'. Luckily, there's another way to work out who is the current Chairman of the (dart) Board, and that's by having a crack at our simple quiz. Don't worry, we've dealt with non-standard boards elsewhere in this book so these questions refer to the boards with which we're all familiar, be they at home or on telly as we cheer on our heroes.

1. What substance are dartboards usually made of in the steel-tip game?

a. Sisal/bristle
b. Wood/shavings
c. Fibreglass/asbestos

2. Name a few other materials for boards you could buy. Point for each.

3. What's the predominate source for the main substance mentioned in question one?

a. Cat hair
b. Agave plant
c. String beans

4. What is a regulation dartboard's diameter?

a. 17¾ inches
b. 18¼ inches
c. 20 inches

5. And how thick is a regulation board, i.e. how far will it stick out from the wall?

a. 6 inches
b. 3 inches
c. 1.5 inches

6. What might you see on a home dartboard (they hold the wires on), but you won't on a competition one?

a. Glue spots
b. Staples
c. Hooks

7. The old, elm-based boards that used to be in most pubs took a beating in the games from all those old, heavy darts. What was the solution to 'healing' these wooden beasts?

a. Overnight soaking to close the puncture holes
b. Hung in a smoker to refresh the top layer
c. Re-carved to produce a brand new top layer

8. When can a competition dartboard be changed? No multiple choice here – a full and complete explanation to get the point, please!

9. And when would the change take place?

a. Immediately
b. After the end of the leg
c. At the end of the set

10. What colour must the 20 segment be, according to the Darts Regulation Authority?

a. Red
b. Green
c. Black

'Bob came on like *The Laughing Cavalier* . . . now he looks like Lee Van Cleef on a bad night.'

WEBCAM DARTS

Yes, you too could spend hours online with a camera pointed at the relevant red bits, fingering your lovely shiny shaft . . . We speak not of OnlyFans but of the phenomenon of webcam darts. With some judicious and honest use of your cam, broadband and your darts skills, you could be touring the world from your games room/bedroom/garage/dartboard stuck to the door of your neighbour's outside toilet while they're at work. So, get ready: warm up those muscles, make sure the lights are at the kind of temperature to ensure things are heating up, and prepare to score a meaty ol' 69 in the company of an eager lonely housewife/husband/furry 12,000 miles away . . .

There are many permutations, but here's a general idea of how to get started.

Choose an app (there are numerous, many free) for your phone/laptop/tablet. You will need an active internet connection to play, so make sure your data is either cheap or you're on Wi-Fi only.

Some apps are self-reporting – you're going to rely on honesty here. At the most basic, player one takes their visit, and inputs their score into the app. Player two then reciprocates. Continue until someone gets the double to finish. Clearly, this is hugely open to manipulation or downright cheating. This is where soft-tip electronic dartboards come into play: some are already hooked up online and some platforms allow you to link your electronic board, which brings accountability.

Other apps involve you pointing your phone at the board from the required official distance. That means, of course, that your actual visit is broadcast live to each other, in which case you've got yourself a game of darts, boyo, and it's a showdown.

Online/webcam darts apps often have competitions and championships, so look out for those. One of the bigger and more organised platforms currently is the Webcam Darts Association, sponsored by Winmau; chat rooms, tourneys, friendly games and statistics at your fingertips are the order of the day. With something like ProDarts you can play against computer opponents, which is good for practice, and Lidarts is another big hitter where the cam is optional. As we say, though, there's loads to choose from – DartConnect and DARTSLIVE come to mind (the latter also offers live darts cricket, for a change of format).

You can of course bypass these official sites entirely

and use whichever messaging app you use the most. This is best for family and friends challenges – and you can choose whichever darts games you fancy playing that day rather than being constrained by the versions of the various sites.

As with online poker, the watchwords here are competitive honesty, with a constant and genuine respect for other players essential. Basically, if you wouldn't do it in a pub league against your rivals, don't do it here: sledging, over-the-top celebrations and aggression are frowned upon (to a point – we're not robots). Enjoying the game while doing everything you can to win is absolutely key: no need to ask or give any quarter when everyone involved is focused and in the zone. When among mates, by contrast, anything goes, doesn't it? Remember you have to face them again at some stage, though, so make sure you can take it if you're gonna dish it out.

Yes, there's no substitute for doing it in person: connecting with another human, maybe both of you getting sweaty as you set your bodies and minds into whichever positions are likely to give you the most pleasure. Tell you what, though: sometimes all that's available is doing it online – and there's absolutely nothing wrong with a bit of cybersix (i.e. double 3 or 2/D2 to finish).

'They won't just have to play outta their skin to beat Phil Taylor. They'll have to play outta their essence.'

'Bristow reasons. Bristow quickens. Aaah, Bristow.'

QUIZ

WHAT'S IN A NAME?

One thing that you absolutely must have as a darts player is a quality nickname. You can't expect to get up there on stage and be taken seriously if you're calling yourself something like Andy 'Pants' Jackson or 'Fluffy Bunnies' Phillipa Jackson (to be fair, those names are quite mild by Jackson standards). Nope, you've got to have something cooler than that, and preferably a moniker that says something about your style of throwing, style of clothes, general appearance, or that simply rhymes neatly with your given name.

It's not necessarily up to you, either – like any nickname in real life, it may well be bestowed on you by well-meaning (or, more likely, piss-taking) mates. Once you've got your darts name in place, it's almost impossible to change, too, so you may well end up being the first Fluffy champion of the world, in which case it's really not going to matter too much by comparison. Here's a list of 80 players and nicknames, both from the classic era and the present day. We've been a pain in the darts again and put the wrong names down by the nicknames – can you match them up correctly? Warning: we've put in some red herrings to throw you off the scent, too!

Try saying the name out loud, with a nickname in between the first name and surname. Does it seem appropriate/funny/a pun/just cool AF? Imagine it being called out by the match referee.

Adam Hunt – Flying Scotsman
Adrian Lewis – The Rebel
Alan Norris – The Bronzed Adonis
Anastasia Dobromyslova – Bertie

Andrew Gilding – Rocky
Andy Boulton – Jackpot
Bob Anderson – Barney
Bobby George – X-Factor
Brendan Dolan – The Nuke
Carlton Wuck – The Phenomenon
Ceri Morgan – The Rocket
Chris Dobey – The Power
Colin Osborne – Goldfinger
Damon Heta – Chizzy
Danny Noppert – The Heat
Daryl Gurney – The Freeze
Dave Chisnall – Superchin
Dennis Priestley – The Hunter
Dimitri van den Bergh – Fireball
Dirk van Duijvenbode – Ozzy
Dylan Slevin – Bobby Dazzler
Eric Bristow – Queen of the Palace
Fallon Sherrock – Dynamite
Gabriel Clemens – The Tunnel
Gary Anderson – The Menace
Gerwyn Price – Titan
Jamie Lewis – The Iceman
Jan Dekker – The Artist

Jeffrey de Graaf – Oceans
Jelle Klaasen – The Ferret
Joe Cullen – Old Stoneface
John Lowe – The Polish Eagle
John Part – The Hulk
Jonny Clayton – Spider
José de Sousa – The Hurricane
Josh Rock – Relentless
Kai Gotthardt – The Crafty Cockney
Keane Barry – The German Giant
Kevin Doets – Marathon Man
Kevin Painter – Double Dekker
Kim Huybrechts – The Dreammaker
Krzysztof Ratajski – The Rock Star
Leighton Rees – Wolfie
Luke Humphries – Historymaker
Luke Littler – Cool Hand Luke
Madars Razma – The Special One
Mark Webster – The Cobra
Martin Adams – The Real Deal
Matt Campbell – Bully Boy
Max Hopp – The Asp
Michael Smith – Mighty Mike
Michael van Gerwen – Hawkeye

Mike De Decker – Ginja Ninja
Mitchell Clegg – The Singapore Slinger
Nathan Aspinall – Maximiser
Paul Lim – The Prince of Wales
Peter Wright – Rapid
Phil Taylor – Pikachu
Raymond van Barneveld – Heavy Metal
Ricardo Pietreczko – Madhouse
Richie Burnett – The Moosta
Ricky Evans – Snakebite
Ritchie Edhouse – Latvian Razzmatazz
Rob Cross – From Russia With Love
Robbie Diebel – The 12-Year-Old Vintage
Rocky Mademann – Hellraiser
Ronnie Baxter – Shaggy
Ross Smith – Voltage
Ryan Joyce – Cool Hand
Ryan Searle – The Wizard
Scott Rand – Hollywood
Scott Williams – Darth Maple
Simon Whitlock – Golden Girl
Stephen Bunting – The Magpie
Stephen Burton – Hawaii 501

Steve Beaton – The Bullet
Trina Gulliver – The Limestone Cowboy
Wayne Mardle – Smudger
William O'Connor – Chuck

'This lad has more checkouts than Tesco.'

'Look at the man go: it's like trying to stop a water buffalo with a pea-shooter.'

QUIZ

IT'S ALL ABOUT THE BOARD

Think you know your way around a dartboard? Well, bully for you – literally, if you go on the revived *Bullseye*. As you'll note from that iconic television show, though, dartboards come in more guises than the familiar competition board. Indeed, Bully's Prize Board aside, there have been oodles of different dartboards used over the years. You'll find some still lurking in the corners of traditional pubs and darts clubs across the UK.

We've put together a few of our favourite different boards. Good luck!

1. This board has standard numbering, but no trebles or outer bull. It was featured more than once on the influential *Indoor League*. But is it:

a. Yorkshire Doubles Dartboard
b. Manchester Legend Board
c. Kent Doubles Board

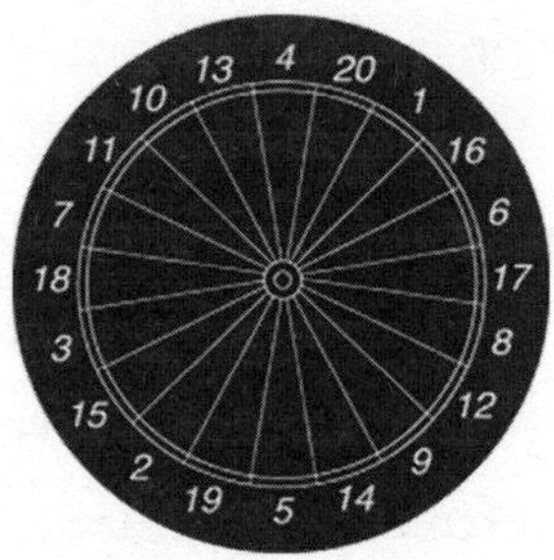

2. The name of this board gives a clue as to what it used to be made from. Again, no trebles, and the numbering is way different to modern competition boards. Want a clue? Cross the Pennines from the previous question!

a. Lincoln Limewood Board
b. Manchester Log-end Dartboard
c. Ironbridge Ironboard

3. Staying with that board, do you know what size the playing surface is?

a. 13¼ inches

b. 15 inches

c. 10 inches

4. What was the predominate (specific) material used to make that board?

a. Ironwood

b. Elm

c. Pastrywood

5. This one – standard numbering but with a huge difference to our familiar competition boards – was introduced in 1992. Simple: name it.

a. Quadro 240

b. Quadboard 2000

c. Four-for-more

6. And what's the top score with three darts on this board?

a. 200

b. 240

c. 300

7. A twofer here – you'll see the numbers on these dartboards are not just repeated, they go up in increments of five. One point for naming each dartboard (clue: named after specific places); another point for knowing the main difference between them; a final point for knowing what specific game is played on them (clue: it's not 501).

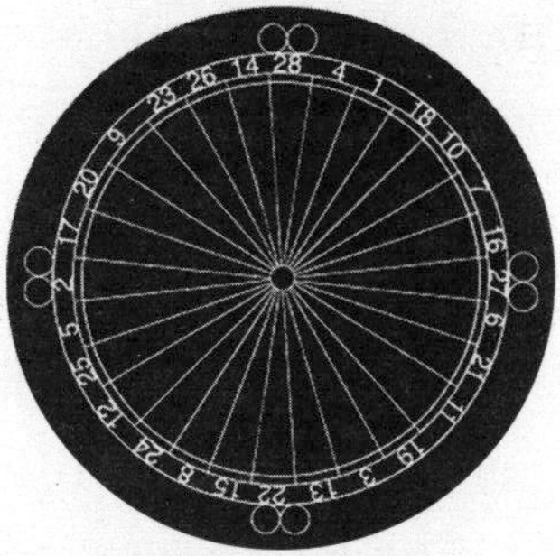

8. Now things are going to get *very* weird and wonderful. Check out this amazing piece of darting history. Where on earth would you find a board like this thing?

a. Grimsby
b. Goole
c. Bangor

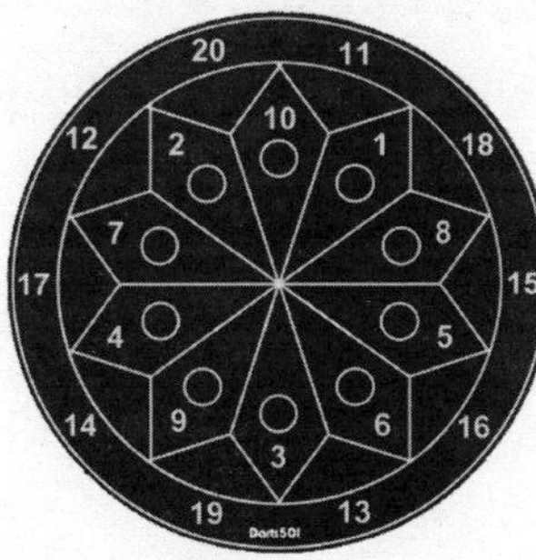

9. This is a real head-scratcher now – going back to the late 1800s, in fact. Which water-named place is the source of this absolute beast of a board?

a. Bath
b. Jacob's Creek
c. Waterville, TN

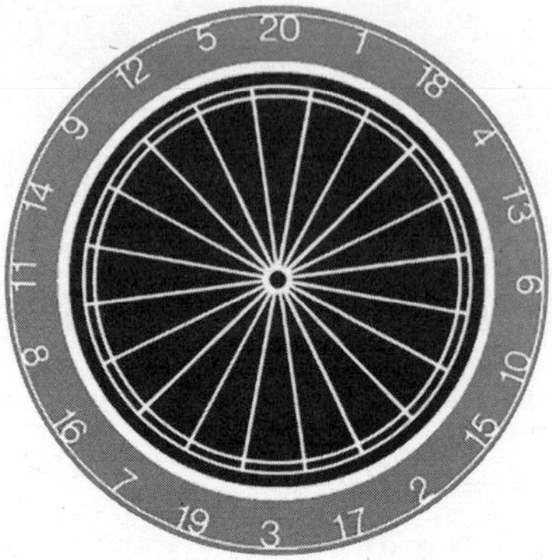

10. This one is said to originate from the board in our first question, as you can see by the lack of trebles and outer bull. Curiously, though, this one's built with an outer and inner ring – the inner ring can turn to enable repositioning of heavily used numbers (and therefore gaining longer use out of the same board, to move what was once e.g. 9 into the 20 spot to refresh it). Name it!

a. Kent Doubles
b. Yorkshire Trebles
c. Cardiff Singles

There are oodles of other boards out there – indeed, it's a fascinating hobby which can get extremely expensive if you start collecting them. The board space, of course, has been long used for advertisements and footy team-themed versions. Which ones are your favourites?

ARROW MAINTENANCE

Don't be that bad worker that always blames their tools . . . your darts are absolutely key and if you don't look after them, they certainly won't look after you. No matter how skilful a player you are, you won't be able to compensate for the erratic trajectory caused by knacked flights, and you will certainly suffer from bounce-outs at the most inopportune of times if you don't take a few moments now and again to assess the performance of your three little friends. Luckily, it's nothing you can't do at home – so here's a few things to look out for in maintaining your arrers.

Keep them in a proper case

If nothing else, it's going to keep your darts together for when you need them. Don't be a scruffbag and have them lying around or loose in your bag or pocket. Not only will they almost certainly poke into your skin at the worst moments, but it also shows you're the kind of person who literally does not care about keeping anything in good nick. As with darts, so with relationships – you're guaranteed not to pull. Seriously, though, don't keep your precious arrows in a dog-poo bag or similar:

get yourself a nice case or wallet to protect them, and to keep spare flights, shafts and maintenance gizmos in. You won't regret it.

Keep it clean

You know how surgeons do that handwashing thing where they get that blue soap stuff and wash right up to their elbows, then hold their arms up weirdly and put on blue gloves? That's to stop gunk getting onto their scalpels, drills and ultimately, patients. We're not suggesting you go quite *that* far before picking up your darts for a game, but the barrels in particular do pick up grot, which affects their performance. Sweat, dead skin cells and whatever you've been plunging your mitts into will all transfer onto the shafts, so get the baby wipes out (and dry them!) and you'll find the grip is just that little bit better.

Keep 'em sharp

Maybe the most important thing to purchase is a dart sharpener. These little tools cost only a couple of quid and can make all the difference – before every match give your darts a good couple of minutes and ensure they retain their sticking power into that board. It's even more important if you're in a pub team and playing away at an unfamiliar venue – you never know how their board is going to react to your style. A dart sharpener, about the same size as a snooker player's chalk, is a vital piece of gear. Blunt darts = losing darts.

It's a wrench

Literally, a wrench tool for a number of purposes. These days there are plenty of different versions of the multitool darts wrench, but most are small and beautiful things that will easily fit in your case. Shop around till you find one you particularly like; with these you can align and tighten the shaft, adjust the tip and generally make fine adjustments to ensure consistency and ultra-straight arrows. You may also want to pair it with a broken-shaft removal tool for those rare and frustrating occasions when things go properly out of control.

Other gizmos

Flight punchers, tip extractors, repointers, pocket scales . . . the choice is yours and the companies will no doubt be happy to sell you as many additional bits and bobs as they can manufacture. So far, though, a 'talent confirmer' is yet to be available, to our dismay.

Dartboard maintenance

- Don't let 'em get wet.
- Don't feed 'em after midnight.
- Never go back to a lighted dartboard.
- The most important thing to know about a traditional dartboard is that you can take off and rotate the number ring. So, when the 20s, 19s, D16/8s get gnarly, you can remove the number ring (retain all screws and whatnot, obviously), rotate the board two or three numbers, and make what used to be 9 or 12 into 20. Ideally, you'd do this after every 20 hours of play, but who the heck is gonna remember to do that? So, once the 20s bed starts looking like a Glastonbury field on day two, take the board down and give it some love, eh? And, seriously, do not let it get wet – it'll expand and contract weirdly when it's dry, and you'll end up with a bumpy board that's no use to man or beast. Any loose fibres – cut 'em off with nail scissors. Half an hour's work is way better than having to buy a brand-new board every few months, after all.

PLAY IT: KILLER

GAME

Players:

Two to 21

In brief:

Qualify as a killer and then kill the other players (by throwing darts at a board, not by throwing darts at the other players, obviously).

How to play:

Each player is designated a number. You can do this by putting numbers 1–20 on small pieces of paper in a bag, hat or empty pint pot and each player picks one out; blindfolded, to avoid the inevitable rush to grab 16s or tops. You could also each throw one dart with your non-throwing hand to secure a number (i.e. left hand if you're usually a right-handed thrower, and vice versa). In this scenario, if someone lands on a number that's already been nabbed, just throw again – you can't grab someone else's number. Each player then has a home number.

Once that's all sorted, it's time to play. Three darts per player per visit. It's a straight knockout, last-player-standing game, and each player begins with three lives.

First, a player must become a killer by hitting the double of their home number three times (carried over across visits). Mark these on the scoreboard and put a K by your name. Once you are a killer you are always a killer and can't lose that status. The aim of the game is for a killer to destroy the other players by hitting the other players' home double (whether they're a qualified killer or not – they may never get to be a killer if they're eliminated first!). Every time that's achieved then the killer has taken a life from that player, which is marked on the scoreboard. Once a player has lost all their three lives they are out of the game. Continue until there's only one player standing. It's absolute mayhem once everyone's a qualified killer! This game's obviously amazing to hone your skills in finishing under pressure.

Friendly fire

Beware: if you inadvertently hit your own home double, you lose one of your own lives. This is particularly dangerous if, for example, your home is on 20 and your mate's is on 5, i.e. next door to yours. Friendly fire can take you down as effectively as the other killers!

Variation one

Up the number of lives everyone starts with for a longer game.

Variation two

Army mode: two teams, of equal numbers of players, all defending one single number and all attacking the opposition's single number.

Variation three

Treble it up: if there's a local pro in the squad, they have to hit trebles both to become a killer and to kill other players. If there's a beginner player in the squad, they only have to hit singles to attain killer status and to kill other players. This makes the game accessible to way more people of all ages, experience and skills.

Variation four

The sniper: first, everyone selects their home numbers. Then each player has one dart to get closest to the inner bull. The one who achieves this is the sniper – the only killer on the board. Everyone else has to defend their number by trying to take out the sniper (hitting three bulls or one double bull and one single in total). Only the sniper may kill the other players . . .

Variation five

Blind killer: for this you will need to agree which numbers are active, according to the number of players. So, if there are five of you then 20, 19, 18, 17, 16 are active and nothing else counts. Write each number on a piece of paper; each player picks their number out of a hat or pint glass, etc., but *does not tell anyone else.* Mark the active numbers on the scoreboard. In this variation nobody starts with a double, so everyone begins a killer – and super-carnage ensues. At the end of the game or when a player is out, they then reveal which number was their home base, though by then it will be fairly clear anyway.

'He's as twitchy as a frog in a blender.'

DARTS LEGEND

Name: John Thomas Wilson

Nickname: Jocky

Date of birth: 22nd March, 1950

Place of birth: Kirkcaldy, Scotland

Died: 24th March, 2012 (age 62)

Active since: 1972; turned professional 1979

Darts: 21g Datadarts; Right-handed

Walk-on music: Survivor: 'Eye of the Tiger'

Shirt: Often two-coloured, sometimes in Scottish-flag blue and white, signature on back

Notable achievements: Double World Championship Winner; twice runner-up in World Masters; numerous wins in other tournaments during 1980s; gold medal with Scotland's men's team in 1987 WDF Europe Cup; two silvers (singles and team) in Europe Cup competitions; eight bronze medals with team, pairs and singles in Europe Cup; quarter-finalist at least in all World Championships from 1979 to 1991 (eight quarters, three semis, two wins); many appearances on *Bullseye*; along with Angus Ross and Rab Smith, his Scotland team beat England 5–4 in 1981's BDO Nations Cup Final (England included his great rival Eric Bristow); hit 240 with three darts in the 'quadruple 20' using the briefly popular quadro board in the WDC Skol UK Matchplay, 1993, where he lost in the final to Dennis Priestley.

Controversies: Ex-miner, coal man, fish worker and British army squaddie, Jocky fought his way up against the odds – he was brought up in an orphanage for large parts of his childhood; known to use the darker arts of psychology by looking his opponents in the eye and showing no fear at all; famously had dentures and no remaining teeth by age 28, a legacy of his habit of chomping on sweets; banned briefly in 1982 for brawling with an official, possibly related to the Falklands War (Jocky's wife was called Malvina, as in 'Las Malvinas', the Argentinian name for the Falklands, and an official had a pop about it, apparently); always a heavy drinker, eventually his diabetes stopped his boozing during matches from 1995 when he finished competing as a pro; declared bankruptcy in 1998 and ended up as something of a hermit from then on, not even giving interviews to the press; eventually his 50-a-day cigarette habit led to chronic obstructive pulmonary disease (2009); died at home aged 62 in Kirkcaldy. In 2009 the PDC ran a tournament called 'The Jocky Wilson Cup' – where England beat Scotland by six points to nil. Oof! And then there's that *Top of the Pops* moment where a giant pic of him appeared behind Dexys Midnight Runners – for their song 'Jackie Wilson Said (I'm in Heaven When You Smile)' . . .

Quote: When asked about why he didn't brush his teeth: 'My gran told me the English poison the water.'

'Steve Beaton – the Adonis of darts, what poise, what elegance – a true Roman gladiator with plenty of hair wax.'

'There hasn't been this much excitement since the Romans fed the Christians to the lions.'

QUIZ

DARTITIS AND OTHER INJURIES

You've practised till your fingers are blue. Your dartboard looks like it's going on holiday to the deepest Amazon basin and has had to have hundreds of injections from the doctor. You're dreaming of your arrows thunking into that treble bed one after the other. You even start to eat food from dartboards instead of proper plates. Yep, you're living the game, and your time has come to step up and show the world what you can do.

Your intro music plays and the crowd roars its approval, quickly joining in with the singalong choruses

like supporters at an FA Cup final. You shake hands with the ref and his team; you shake hands with your opponent. Both of you chuck a few practice darts at the board. Then, the ref quietens the arena with those magic words: game on.

You walk up to the oche the exact same way you have a thousand times before. Your laser glare is set right at that treble 20 bed. You aim your first dart, draw back your arm and . . . nothing happens. You try again. Look, aim, draw back hand . . . nothing. The sickening feeling begins in your stomach as you start to sweat, glancing around you as the murmurs of a questioning packed-out crowd pierce your concentration. You breathe out, gather yourself, step back, start your preparation again.

But you cannot let go of the dart.

You are Eric Bristow, one of the greatest players ever to take up the game, and you are suffering from a debilitating condition.

You have dartitis.

Dartitis is best described as an arrows version of the yips in golf. In both cases, there is nothing physically awry – you can be in the absolutely greatest shape of your life, but when it comes to the crunch moment something stops you following through your movements even though you've practised them a million times. It's a kind of tension, a twitch, something psychological that creeps in and wrecks your game. What now?

For Bristow, it took 10 years to work through it – he even re-attained his number one world status. Others who've suffered from dartitis include the former world champ Mark Webster, multiple women's world champ Beau Greaves, Berry van Peer and Nathan 'The Asp' Aspinall.

Van Peer later told the *Sun* that he has learned to deal with the affliction by a mixture of practise, positive thinking, visualisation and removing negative thoughts. 'Breathing patterns have helped a little bit too. Confidence is a lot, especially mentally,' he said. Van Peer also reported that he was in an over-heightened state of alertness, in which something like a friend walking past while he was playing would pop his bubble of concentration completely. The Asp, meanwhile, said he had developed a fear of missing, which stopped him in his tracks. He'd compose himself by taking deep breaths.

According to Kevin 'The Artist' Painter, his own bout with dartitis was brought on by anxiety and stress. He has taken sessions of hypnotherapy with

Chris O'Connor, the official hypnotherapy partner of the Professional Darts Players Association. It's based on visualisation, confidence and motivation work – techniques that sufferers can learn and implement to calm the racing mind. O'Connor has worked with over 50 dartitis sufferers, plus world champions in snooker and even UFC fighters. Painter said he also started drinking less while playing, which has helped him retain a clear head. Darts without a pint? Gotta be worth a try – particularly when the stakes are high. Dartitis is no respecter of talent; indeed, the pressure on the top players is enough to make them think twice about what should be second nature.

If it's something that bothers you then don't suffer in silence – psychology is there for everyone to tap into. There's no shame in asking for help and it'll make you a better player at the end of the day.

Keeping relatively fit is also more important than you might think. Yes, there are more physically taxing sports than one that requires you stand up and lob stuff at a board, but the repeated movements of darts are also going to lead to strains if you're not careful. Anything that affects your stance or throwing action is gonna put you off your game; and obviously, your eyesight is another key aspect, so get down to the optician and have that test you've been putting off for months.

Whose Injury?

Match the injury to the darts player – all these are actual real-life incidents, on and off the oche! Again, we've mixed 'em up for you to sort out.

Peter Wright – shoulder injury due to cutting down trees
Nathan Aspinall – stung by wasp
Jelle Klaasen – gallstones
Simon Whitlock – neck injury
Adam Smith-Neale – hole in wrist tendon
Alan Warriner-Little – pierced finger in left hand due to catching bounce-out
Darius Labanauskas – neck injury after putting shirt on shirt wrongly
Luke Littler – broken leg
Jermaine Wattimena – double fracture of collarbone in Belgian Cup Final fans' dust-up
Kim Huybrechts – injured index finger in non-throwing hand due to ham-carving injury on Christmas Day

Michael van Gerwen – rolled ankle due to being jumped on by Adam Smith-Neale
Gary Anderson – tendonitis in wrist

'Tarantino re-writing *Gunfight at the O.K. Corral* couldn't have done any better than this.'

CALCULATING YOUR AVERAGE

It's a simple calculation but there's a couple of things to remember when calculating your three-dart average.

The easiest way to do this is the one used most often: divide 501 by the total number of darts used to get there. This includes finishes and doubles, and makes today's averages of 110+ even more impressive.

Here's some other ways to think about it, which will help you as a player calculate how strong your *scoring* average is, with figures in our system not including finishes. Not standard, we know, but we reckon it's more useful.

Part one: get the single-dart average

Firstly, disregard any darts after you've set up a finish. So, anything under 170 excluding the bogey numbers (169, 168, 166, 165, 163, 162 and 159) is not included in your average score. What we're after here is simply how many points you're regularly getting with your score-building arrows.

Take your remaining score – 331, for example, if you've left 170 – and divide it by the number of darts it's taken you to get there. Yesterday I did this and it took me eight darts to get to that 170 (honest). So, 331 ÷ 8 is the equation. I can't work that out in my head so the calculator says: 41.375.

Three-dart average revealed

That makes my single-dart average score a healthy 41.375. Times that by three to get the three-dart average and again my calculator gives the result: 124.125. So my three-dart average for that leg was pretty much higher than any professional darts player you could name.

Let's do it with 18 – a more sensible amount of darts: 331 ÷ 18 = 18.388. Times that by three to get the three-dart average and you'll get 55.166, which is a very decent amateur darts player's average score.

OK, OK, OK, let's be *actually in real life accurate to my actual game* and divide 331 by the *real* number of darts it'd probably take me, which is more like 28 on a bad day. So, to get to the single-dart average we divide my score by the number of darts: 331 ÷ 28 = 11.821. Multiply that by three to get my three-dart average for that leg and it's 35.464, which I have to fess up to, folks. Darts is a cruel game; no matter how much you love it, it doesn't mean you're any good at it (a bit like sex).

That's just one leg of darts – to get the set scores you can either total the entire scores over the set (minus finishes) then divide by the total number of darts in the entire set (to get the single-dart average) then multiply by three to get the set average; or you can do it as above, leg by leg. In the second calculation you'll then have to add up all the single-leg averages together and divide by the number of legs.

As we say, the much more depressing way to do it is, rather than ignoring any *possible* finish, you must include any darts taken before you *actually* finish. This of course is going to drag down your average as well as send your self-worth right into the khazi, so we really don't advise going anywhere near it. Our way is the one that makes us feel a bit less like total losers, so we're sticking with it – until we go pro, anyway.

I FEEL THE NEED . . . THE NEED FOR SPEED (DARTS)

Eventually, every sport comes down to seeing who can do it the fastest – even chess, that mighty meeting of minds, has a version where you're restricted in the amount of time taken to make your move. Darts is no exception, and the PDC's version is a bit daft but a lot of fun – speed darts.

Essentially, it's a challenge to a selected top player, based around 501, in order to get to a finish as quick as possible. To help them on their way said player is asked a series of questions first, and getting a correct answer gives them 50 points. Those 50 points are taken off the 501, making it progressively easier to complete the task. It's a bit of fun, rather than any kind of official contest (for now, anyway). That contest was version 2.0 – we love the idea of that, so we've put a version together below. Go online and you can see Gerwyn Price et al. give that a bash.

It was followed in 2025 by a new format involving a new clutch of players from Rob Cross to Leonard Gates, Ross Smith to Martin Lukeman as they all try their luck. This time around, the player on the oche has a minute and a half to basically pile on as many points as possible – no questions here, simply get those arrows chucked into the board. We encourage you to play that one too – all you need is a stopwatch and a bunch of mates willing to give it a good old go. You might wanna add forfeits and/or prizes for slowest and/or fastest – maybe the worst player buys a round. Maybe the best player has to down a pint before the next round-robin game begins. Up to you!

GAME

Here's our versions of speed darts . . .

Speed darts one

You will need: a question master (with a stopwatch and some questions – use this book!), some players and a dartboard set-up.

How to play

First, divide the number of questions by the number of players. If there's two players, it's five questions each; if there's three, three questions each (and one as a tiebreak if needed); four players, two questions each (two tiebreakers). Each player has (for example) one and a half minutes in total.

The question-meister asks a question.

If the darts player gets the question correct, they go for a board visit, with their score recorded. Another question is then asked, and so on until the time runs out. If questions run out before time does, the player can go to the board again and try to improve their score.

If they do not get the question right, they are penalised 30 seconds before their visit. Return, another question is asked, and so on until time runs out as above. Highest score wins!

Variation

Get fiendish – nobody can visit the board until they've got a question right, so their time will tick away until they've answered something correctly!

You can set the timer to whatever you like: one and a half minutes is only a suggestion as it makes for a ridiculously fast game. As the night wears on you're probably gonna want to extend that time as asking the questions will take longer, as will answering them.

Speed darts two

How to play

Agree a maximum time beforehand for each player. In this version, there's no questions – simply pure darts challenge.

The player then has to get down from 301 (including a double finish) in that time. Any time left in seconds is their score for that round. Note that if the clock runs out before they finish they may continue to play, but can only score a maximum of one single point. The highest score wins that leg (i.e. the longest time left on the clock so the fastest checkout).

Variation

Use 501, or 101, or 1001, or . . .

Speed darts three

How to play

Each player has, for example, a minute and a half to score as many points as possible from as many visits as they can fit into their 90 seconds. Highest score is the winner.

We're pretty sure that Terry Down isn't going to pull up any trees in these games, but if it was a contest of *slow darts* then there'd be only one winner. To each their own, and to the winner the spoils. Have fun, folks, and please remember to stand well clear of the board in this one – fast the throwing may be, but more accurate it probably will not be. That said, it's not a bad way to find your ideal throwing speed, because it's all about the points accrued.

Your whole darts-throwing process might well be too slow (or too fast), so while speed darts might seem a little extreme at first it does reward you playing *at a speed that's fast enough to retain the maximum accuracy*. And that, ladies and gents, is what arrows is ultimately all about.

PLAY IT: SHANGHAI

GAME

Players:

From one to everyone

In brief:

Hit each target number single, double and treble before moving on.

How to play:

Start at 1 and move round the board per turn. That is, after *everyone* has had a chance to Shanghai on 1, then move to 2 for the next visit; even if one player has already Shanghai-ed, everyone completes a visit on that turn. Tot up your scores exactly as per the darts that score, so if you get a double 1 and a treble 1 on your first visit that's 5 points. If your opponent does not score then they get no points, but you still move up to try and score on number 2 for the next visit. This moves the game along swiftly. Ends when everyone has had a chance to hit the bull. The winner is the one with the highest cumulative score.

Variation one

A player may not move on until they have Shanghai-ed each number. Therefore, some players may be aiming to, say, Shanghai 6 while player one is still stuck on 1. In this variation you can carry your attempts over; so, if player one scores a double and a single on their visit, all they need to hit is the treble of that same number on their next visit, then they can move on to the next number. This is a much longer game.

Variation two

Start the game from 12 upwards, or agree to only play even or odd numbers, or any other version you can think of.

Variation three

Instant Shanghai: if any player Shanghai-es any of their numbers on a single visit, they win the game. So, theoretically you could go first, and hit single, double and treble 1. That's a Shanghai in the truest sense, as pure as you get. Bit annoying for other players, mind you, but you could always start again.

Variation four

Knockout. If you have several players, continue as variation three – but carry on with all the rest of the contenders. You're now playing for second place, then third, etc. If you're really fiendish you can make the last player carry on until they get any Shanghai at all, which means the game could literally go on forever. (You probably want to get a second dartboard set up as well if you're gonna go down this route, so all the other better players don't get bored and wander off to play pool or shove ha'penny or *GTA* or something.)

Variation five

Handicap. Obviously, we're all at different skill levels here so to make it competitive, different players start at different numbers. The best player has to start from 1, of course. But other players might have a handicap of 5, so begin at 5, or a handicap of 9, so begin at 9. The chase is on! And, yes, you might have a complete novice who you handicap at bull while the best player's on 1 – and the best player may well still win. Do you accept the challenge?

Variation six

Finish it. You will quite often see players try to Shanghai a finish – 120 is a popular one – and finishing, as you would, on a double. For this variation play only three-dart finishes that you might encounter during an actual game of 501. You can calculate a Shanghai easily by multiplying the single score by six, by the way (and, conversely, find the root single by dividing the total by six).

Here's a few for you to start with: 114 (19s); 108 (18s); 102 (17s); 96 (16s); 90 (15s); 84 (14s); 78 (13s) . . . unlikely you'll ever want to do a three-dart finish for a score of 6, but if you do, it's Shanghai on the number 1. This practice game gives you two darts to set up the double, so you can choose to carry your scores over to the next visit as you would in a competitive game, and of course if you bust yourself, your score goes back up to the target Shanghai.

QUIZ

NINE-DART HEROES

It's the greatest achievement in any single leg of darts – to finish in the smallest number of arrows possible. That is, to get from 501 to 0, finishing on a double, in a mere three visits to the oche. The nine-dart finish has been achieved numerous times and we've been fortunate enough that many of them have been televised. That not only means that we're able to rewatch the stunning moments when someone has been touched by the hand of genius, but also we've got evidence of it – something our dodgy mate Whistlin' Jeff is sadly lacking in his tales of his own so-called nine-darters. Here's a few questions for you on this most wonderful of darting achievements.

1. How many different 141 outshots do we normally see for a nine-darter?

a. 2

b. 3

c. 4

2. A point each: name them.

3. You can achieve a nine-darter with the same score for each of your three visits. How so?

4. In 2025, Luke Littler hit a nine-darter in Cardiff in the Premier League. What was his unusual outshot?

5. Why was his performance that night – in the fourth leg of the final of Night Seven – also unexpected?

a. He hadn't practised for a week

b. He was playing with someone else's darts

c. He was playing with a broken toe

6. Who was he playing against that night?

a. Luke Humphries

b. Michael van Gerwen

c. Cliff Lazarenko

7. How many different combinations are there to get 501 in nine darts?

a. 15
b. 9,100
c. 3, 944

8. And how many of those fulfil the criteria for a double-in and double-out match?

a. 14
b. 8,190
c. 574

9. Which player scored the first televised nine-darter?

a. Eric Bristow
b. Jocky Wilson
c. John Lowe

10. And did that player give us all a huge grin?

a. Never
b. No chance
c. Nope

'Keith Deller is like Long John Silver – he's badly in need of another leg.'

'Steve Beaton, he's not Adonis, he's the donis.'

QUIZ

ONE HUNDRED AND EIIIIIIIIIGHTY

Yes, it's doubles that win matches, but a maximum score of 180 gets everyone going: the announcer, the crowd, the ref, the players, the viewers at home. You can't hide up there on stage; the top players expect to get a ton-eighty every time they step up to the oche (apart from when trying to finish, obviously). Let's have a delve into this most thrilling of moments and see if we can ruin it by over-analysis.

1. In a multi-leg set under tournament 501 rules, what is the maximum number of 180s a player can throw in a row?

a. 2
b. 3
c. 4

2. And how many treble 20s can be thrown in a row?

a. 14
b. 13
c. 12

3. In what year was the first televised 180 by a man?

a. 1990
b. 1983
c. 1973

4. And which player achieved the feat?

a. Alan Evans
b. Gerwyn Price
c. Eric Bristow

5. What was significant about that player's status?

a. He had never played darts before

b. He was an amateur

c. He threw them underarm

6. Which year saw the first televised 180 by a woman?

a. 1988

b. 2018

c. 1977

7. And what was that player's name?

a. Sandra Gibb

b. Sandy Gee

c. Sandy Cheeks

8. Where is she from?

a. West Newark

b. South Wales

c. North Patagonia

9. And how quick were they to throw all three darts?

a. 2.16 seconds

b. 3.21 seconds

c. 1.80 seconds

10. Who is widely considered to hold the record for fastest 180 scored?

a. Fallon Sherrock
b. Scott Rand
c. Ricky Evans

11. Somewhat unsurprisingly, what's that player's nickname?

a. 'Fast' Fallon Sherrock
b. 'Speedy' Scotty Rand
c. Ricky 'Rapid' Evans

12. What's the secret to getting a 180 every time?

a. Change every number to 20 on the board when nobody's looking, and make the treble beds massive
b. Practice
c. Not telling you, it's a secret

JOCKY WILSON: *TOP OF THE POPS*

Dexys Midnight Runners are a brilliant Celtic folk soul-pop band, whose huge hit 'Come On Eileen' is a staple of any knees-up worth its salt. Their heyday was the late 1970s and early 1980s, with denim dungaree-clad frontman Kevin Rowland a charismatic talisman.

So why on earth did they appear on *Top of the Pops* on 30th September, 1982, in front of an enormous photograph of Fife's finest darts hero, Jocky Wilson?

What an embarrassment for the BBC it must have been – Dexys were actually there to perform their latest single called 'Jackie Wilson Said (I'm in Heaven When You Smile)'. Someone must have misheard the phone call when Dexys told them what they needed that night.

Now, Jackie Wilson was an African-American rhythm and blues hero of the 1950s, with pompadour-slick hair and a wonderful doo-wop voice. His near-namesake, Jocky, was a beer-swigging, diminutive Scotsman with missing teeth who had won the 1982 World Championship of darts, beating John Lowe 5–3 in a thrilling final.

Someone surely was for the chop after confusing the

two men in front of several million avid viewers of the UK's foremost music programme – or not, as it turned out. Rather than it being an error for the ages, it was in fact deliberate. Rowland told the *Guardian* in 2002 that it was absolutely, definitively and totally a joke by the band. 'For a laugh, we told the producer to put a picture of Jocky Wilson up behind us,' he said. The producer replied that people would think it was a BBC boo-boo. 'Only an idiot would think that,' said Rowland.

Either way, it's a brilliant story. 'Jackie Wilson Said' got to number five in the charts, and loads of people got to eat their chippy tea while staring at a 20ft picture of the darts hero Jocky. In any case, when Jocky gave that famous gap-toothed grin, you couldn't help but smile along. Brilliantly, it's very possible that Jackie – the singer – may have even seen the show as he was still very much alive at the time. Sadly, he passed away at age 49 in 1984. There are no extant records of his pub darts average, but we reckon it's probably better than good old Jocky's singing voice.

THE OLD ONES ARE THE BEST ONES: WORLD SENIORS DARTS

The headlines may be full of the likes of Luke Littler and upcoming ridiculously young darts heroes, but what of the more experienced players?

It's not football, where anyone over the age of about 30 is starting to be called a 'veteran', and someone still playing at the unheard-of ancient age of 40 is an absolute outlier. Nope, darts is a game for all ages. Obviously, the years do take their toll – things like eyesight and stamina make it important to keep on top of your health as a player – but fundamentally there's no reason why anyone can't keep thrilling crowds with their accuracy and flair throughout their lives.

To prove it, in 2022 the World Seniors Darts Championship was set up. It was a collaboration between MODUS Sports and Jason Francis, who had previous to draw upon as they'd done something similar with legends of the snooker table and was open to players over the age of 50. Held at the Circus Tavern in Purfleet, the event included no less than 11 former world champions of either the PDC or BDO schools. Indeed, as time goes by the number of players who can say they'd ever been part of the BDO set-up at all is going to fall naturally, so that in itself was a massive point of interest. Invited players included John Lowe, Trina Gulliver and the one and only Phil Taylor, the proud owner of 16 world titles on his own.

As it turned out, The Power was knocked out in the quarters by Kevin Painter. The Artist – who grabbed himself a 170 finish during the championship – went on to lose in the semis to eventual winner, Scotsman Robert Thornton. Thornton defeated Martin Adams by 5–1 in the final, boasting a not-too-shabby average of 92.66 in the process. He also trousered a rather nice £30k for his troubles – Wolfie's runner-up purse was not to be sniffed at either (£12,500).

The Thorn stormed the 2023 event, too, this time defeating Richie Howson by five sets to two. However, Rob's reign finished swiftly the following year as he lost 3–2 to Andy Hamilton in the second round. The title stayed in Scotland, however, with John Henderson whitewashing Colin McGarry in the final. That year it was specified that no PDC tour card holder could enter, making it truly a test of past legends. Probably the performance of the tournament as a whole was that of Lisa Ashton, who put together a very fine run of results including defeating Chris Mason, Scott Mitchell and Michael Huntley to reach the semis, where McGarry squeezed through against The Lancashire Rose by three sets to two.

A change of sponsor from Jennings Bet to BetGoodwin heralded the 2025 edition where – slightly controversially – players without the PDC Tour Card, but aged only 45 or over and therefore virtually babies, were now eligible. Ross Montgomery came up trumps in this one, defeating Gulliver, John Part, Steve Beaton and former champ Robert Thornton along the way. Ross The Boss beat Graham Usher 5–1 in the final, after Usher had laid waste to Derek Coulson, Leonard Gates, Neil Duff and Richard-Eirig Rowlands to get to that stage. (Reigning champ Henderson fell to Coulson in the quarters.)

As well as the World Championships, there's the World Seniors Darts Matchplay to get your fix of the more mature arrows players. Since 2022, champions have been Robert Thornton (2022), Leonard Gates (2023) and John Henderson (2024). You'll have to check the schedules for details of the Matchplay –

it's moved around the calendar a little since its inception.

As for the whippersnappers dominating the sport in their 20s, 30s and even teens – they've a long way to go and a lot to learn before going toe-to-toe with the old guard. The averages and checkouts may be more exciting on the day-to-day PDC tour – but the competition at seniors level is no less intense, and winning means just as much to them as it does anyone else. Long may it be the case – darts is truly the game for all.

'His eyes are bulging like the belly of a hungry chaffinch.'

MAKE YOUR OWN DARTS CARDS

One for a rainy day when the telly's not working, the internet's knackered and you've already arranged all the tins in your food cupboard in alphabetical order.

There's a card game – hugely popular, we might add – which is often under the trademark of Top Trumps (but not exclusively). Essentially, it's a multiplayer game in which all the cards are dealt equally to all players. On the front of the cards is a picture of, say, a character, monster, or sportsperson, with four or five different attributes that are each marked out of 100. The aim of the game is to read out the highest-value attribute from your top card only, and hope that it beats the best in that category from your opponents' cards. In that case, you win all their cards and add them to your pack (if someone else has the highest card, they win the cards, and it becomes their turn). The winner is the one with all the cards at the end of the game. If the category attribute is drawn, the active cards are put in the middle and the attribute of the next card is then compared, and so on until someone wins.

Of course, there are many sets of cards you can buy

that already have darts players as their theme, including current and classic players. But what they do not have, folks, is the likes of you and I. That's where our game comes in, because we're gonna make a darts cards game of our own, based slightly on the same theory as the games we've talked about, but juuust far enough away from them to avoid any copyright issues. Let's call it, oh, I dunno, *Best Bumps*. That should fool the lawyers.

You will need:

Enough blank cards for all the darts players you know (feel free to make some up, too. The nicknames are often the best bit to create.)

How to create the cards:

Select four attributes essential to darts playing. We suggest you choose from things like: scoring ability; finishing; sticking tongue out when aiming; complaining about bounce-outs; wearing bad shirts; all the gear no idea; boasting about ability; actual ability; avoiding buying rounds . . . there's oodles more so make them suitable to your mates. Once you've agreed four categories to go on the cards, it's time to populate them. If you have photos of each player, print them out and stick them to the card – or draw a caricature of them – and remember to use the player's name and nickname. Give each player points out of 100 for each category. It's probably best not to do your own, to be fair – and don't over- or under-mark too much. We suggest you need around a minimum 25 cards in all for a quick-fire game, so it will be a good idea to add some classic darts players or Teletubbies or entirely made-up characters to the set.

Once that's all done – play, as above.

Variation

Forfeits are always fun. First to go out has to make a cup of tea or toast for everyone, or perhaps speak like Sid Waddell for the rest of the game. We're sure you can find some good tasks for the losers. Have fun!

To start you off, we've put together some profiles of five legendary players that are scattered throughout the book to help you with some of the info you might want to include on your *Best Bumps* – so that's a good start for your new game already.

More cards for the set

Here's some more legends' names to conjure with for your new set . . . what strengths do they have? What weaknesses? Be honest on the new set of cards – we can't have every player being 100 per cent on every different category otherwise we'll all win every game and everyone will be happy and go on to live in a world of peace and harmony where the concept of someone losing on the turn of a single piece of paper will be banished forever, lions will lie with lambs, and Bobby George will eschew the bling for a tie-dyed kaftan and a suspiciously large rolled cigarette . . .

Adrian Lewis
Martin Adams
John Part
Raymond van Barneveld
Trina Gulliver
Deta Hedman
Andy Fordham
Dennis Priestley
Bob Anderson
Leighton Rees
Cliff Lazarenko

Ronnie Baxter
Keith Deller
Paul Lim
Mervyn King
Steve Beaton
John Henderson

'That's like giving Dracula the keys to the blood bank.'

PLAY IT: FIVES

GAME

Also known as:
All fives, fivers, 51 by 5s

Players:
Unlimited

In brief:
Score a total of 51 'fives'.

How to play:
The entire standard board is active. To earn points, your total score in your three-dart visit must be divisible by five. For example: player one scores 100. Divide this by 5 and your score for that round is 20 (a great score); player two scores 35 (divide by 5, points scored = 7); player three hits a whopping 177 in their three darts – but as it cannot be divided by 5, in this game they score nil for that round of visits. Continue playing until

someone gets up to 51 game points (that is, their total cumulative score will divide exactly by 5 to make 51 and vice versa). To put it another way, the aim of the game is to be the first to score a total of 255 points, in whatever configuration (51x5). It's an excellent test not only of your darts skills but also your dart maths. And, yes, the bull absolutely counts – three of those lovely inner bulls takes you immediately up to a score of 30. Current darts players are much more enamoured of the high points of the bullseye than in previous years, so it's a very useful skill to have. The advantage, of course, is that you cannot bust your score unless it is agreed before the game that you must score *exactly* 51 fives and no more.

Variation one

Fives is clearly going to make you favour multiples of 5, therefore effectively a useful practice for 5, 10, 15, 20, bull. Change it up by using a different multiplier; you might want to set something up as 41 by 4s, that is, any score divisible by four counts. This is a big help for working on the 16/8/4/2/1 finishing sequence; as you get better and better, you can up the multiplier to 8, and so on. Go around the board with this and your knowledge of doubles will improve game by game.

Variation two

Use only doubles to achieve your scores. This makes it an absolute winner for finishing practice; in the original fives you'll work mostly on tops and 10s, with the odd double 5 sneaking in there.

Variation three

Trebles only. Once you're at this level it could be a very, very quick game indeed, unless you up the required winning amount accordingly – 51 trebles is the same as 153 fives, for example.

Variation four

All three darts on the winning visit must be scoring darts. That means you'll have to set yourself up for a finish that is divisible by five. This can play absolute havoc even with the best players: if you have agreed that the bust rule applies, you've got some serious work to do if you leave yourself on a low amount of fives to get. If you've reached 49 or 50 fives, you'll be having to finish with exactly 10 or exactly 5 with three scoring darts so you'll be mopping up the small beer numbers and nobody wants to be in that place at the end of any kind of darts game. It's embarrassing to be a professional player who ends up needing double 2 or D1 at the end of a 501, but we all have to start somewhere, and as ever, whichever way you find to win is forgotten when you hear the cries of 'game shot' . . .

Feel free to use calculators/phone apps to keep score, but also make sure you write the scores down on the board. If player one scores 25, then write '25' on the board and next to it a 5 (25 = 5) as that indicates the amount of fives player one is on. The more you play, the better your arithmetic will get, which is a huge part of the whole idea.

Being in a pub which serves beer can not only affect your aim but also affect your counting. Make sure everyone's happy with the sums you do before you move on to someone else's turn, for the sake of Zeus.

DARTS LEGEND

Name: John Lowe, MBE (awarded 2019)

Nickname: Old Stoneface

Date of birth: 21st July, 1945

Place of birth: New Tupton, Derbyshire

Active since: 1966; turned pro around 1975

Darts: 21g Unicorn 'John Lowe'; Phase 3, 90 per cent gold; Right-handed

Walk-on music: Whitesnake: 'Here I Go Again'

Shirt: Various colours, usually collared and with his signature and sponsors visible, often made of cotton rather than silk. Not a fan of the flashy style as worn by contemporaries including Bobby George, Eric Bristow, etc.

Notable achievements: Winner of the World Championship in the 1970s, 1980s and 1990s; double World Masters Winner; numerous other wins worldwide in the 1970s, 1980s and 1990s; first televised nine-dart finish (1984); unbeaten as WDF England captain during his tenure, 1986–1993; Secretary of the World Professional Dart Players Association (later PDA); five times BDO British Pentathlon winner; regular member of WDF World Cup teams and as an individual; 25 BDO major finals, with nine wins; six WDF major finals with five wins; author of the influential book *The Art of Darts* (later also an iPhone app).

Controversies: Called out Gerwyn Price's ear defenders for turning darts into a 'pantomime' – said Price had been 'outclassed on stage' by opponent Gabriel Clemens and that Price had 'his own karma at fault' (2023); in the latter days of the BDO World Championship he called it a 'scam' as there was no clarity over what actual prize money was at stake: 'I noticed the title, the BDO World Darts Championship, and that may be the clue, the word "Professional" is not included – professionals play for money, it is their livelihood, honesty and integrity has somehow been overlooked'; said Luke Littler did not have natural ability but because he had been playing since 18 months old it was more 'what he's grown up with' (*Darts Kings* documentary, 2025), and explained that Littler's folks had helped their son's development hugely by putting the board at a suitable height for the youngster rather than making him throw upwards onto a standard dartboard; not his fault, this one, but hilariously in 2022 due to a Google glitch, the then-76-year-old Lowe ended up being listed as a forward in the Norwich City squad – instead of 18-year-old tyro Jonathan Rowe – shades of Dexys and Jocky Wilson there . . .

Quote: When talking about his nine-dart finish: 'Not luck. Nineteen years of practice.'

PLAY IT: CRICKET

GAME

Also known as:

cut-throat, English cricket, batters

Players:

Two upwards; multiple teams of equal numbers

In brief:

'Open' and 'close-out' numbers and score as much as you can.

How to play:

Multiple teams of players, taking it in turn. The scoring zone comprises 15–20 plus bull.

At the start of the game, each number is closed and cannot be scored from until a player has hit it three times. For example, once player one has hit 3 x 17, they have opened that number and may score from it counting up from zero. Nobody else can score from 17, but they can close it by hitting it three times themselves. Once closed, numbers cannot be opened again.

Scoring:

Doubles count as two hits, trebles as three – so if player one hits treble 17 on their first dart they can score from it immediately. You cannot self-close a number once you've opened it, so you may score from that number unlimited times until it is closed off by other players. The winner has the highest score after all numbers have been opened and then closed. Keep a record of each player/team's hits on the chalkboard otherwise there will be biiiiig trouble, trust me.

Variation one

Widen the scoring area to numbers 10 to 20.

Cut-throat variation

In a two-player or two-team challenge, the points you score when a number is open are credited to the opponents' team. The winners are the ones with the lowest score once all scoring numbers have been closed off.

Variation two

Defensive cricket. Team one is the defending side, and team two is the scoring side. In this version, all scoring numbers are open at the start of the game. The defenders hitting the target thrice means the number is closed, while team two, the scorers, must score as much as possible before all the numbers are closed. Note that team one cannot score and team two does not need to open numbers and cannot close them. After all have visited the board, the teams swap so team two are defenders and team one scorers. Highest score after each has had a turn both as defenders and scorers wins.

Variation three

I've got something to declare (aka English cricket/batters). Team one are defenders (bowlers) and team two scorers (batters). Every number on the board is active. Proceed with scoring as in variation two, but here the defensive team's target is taking 10 wickets, that is, closing out three scoring numbers. Teams swap after an innings, and the highest scorers after each has batted wins.

You can of course have multiple innings in the vein of a Test match, though rain is unlikely to stop play here.

Continuing with the cricket theme, if a team is in bat and reckon they've built up a big enough score, they can 'declare' and put the other team into bat. Likewise, if a team in their first innings has not scored the required amount, they must 'follow-on', that is, go into bat again straight away. Please don't ask us to explain how the follow-on works, 'cause we've got a lot more experience of the follow-through around here, sadly. Note: you can handicap scores so the first, say, 30 points scored in a number don't count, although all that really does is close off scoring for numbers 1–10. Up to you.

'The players are under so much duress, it's like Duressic Park out there.'

THE DARTS CELEBRATION

You might see footballers do this once they've scored a goal . . .

It's all James Maddison's fault, y'know. The Spurs ace is prone to celebrating goals by miming chucking darts into a board. It's caught on big-style and many of his teammates, including Son Heung-min, have joined in. Welsh international teammate Brennan Johnson's also been seen on camera doing the darts celebration.

Maddison is a keen darts player and practises at home, and said that he'd often play with teammates over the years from his various clubs including Jamie Vardy and Harvey Barnes. As footballers have downtime, particularly in away matches, the dartboard would go up and competitions would begin.

Though Maddison plays for Spurs, it was Arsenal superstar Bukayo Saka who gave us his very best MVG impersonation during a North London derby, in September 2023. Apparently, though, it was just a bit of banter between international teammates.

Things weren't quite so friendly when Neal Maupay wound up Spurs fans by doing his own impression of the darts celebration, when he scored for Brentford at Tottenham in January 2024 to put the Bees 2–0 up. Maupay is one of the sport's chief wind-up merchants and delights in the dark arts of getting inside people's heads – but the joke was on him as Maddison and Spurs turned things round to win 3–2. And, yes, Maddison did perform the celebration in response. What goes around, comes around . . .

So now the darts are out of the bag, so to speak, loads of players are prone to use the celebration – Donyell Malen (then of Borussia Dortmund) has been known to do so, which is not a surprise given how big darts is in his home country of the Netherlands.

It works the other way around, too, of course: Luke Littler, during the last-eight match against Nathan Aspinall at Ally Pally in January 2025, gave the crowd his best version of Didier Drogba's two-arms-out, swan-like celebration. The Nuke said his mate had been on at him to do it at some stage after seeing Drogba's antics on *FIFA*. Well, it's better than that boring Alan Shearer one-arm-in-the-air one, at least.

As is the nature of these things, the James Maddison darts celebration is available to you in EA Sports' *FC25*: after you've smashed one into the onion bag, hold down

RT and spin the right analog stick anti-clockwise. We promise it won't wind up your opponents at all.

'As they say at the DHSS, we're getting the full benefit here.'

'This game of darts is twisting like a rattlesnake with a hernia.'

DARTS FOR ALL

The world of darts is becoming more and more inclusive by the year with disability groups and governing bodies working hard on bringing the game to everyone.

However, there's still a way to go: according to the Equality and Human Rights Commission, 20 per cent of venues are not conducive to access by wheelchairs. Similarly, there needs to be more consideration of elements including adaptive equipment for players; the governing bodies, whether BDO or PDC, need to move quickly to include everyone who's interested in the wonderful sport, and that means talking to the people involved.

In 2014 the WDF did just that, approving a set-up for disabled players that included a new measurement of the bull to the ground – 137cm – which is hugely more suitable for wheelchair users.

World Disability Darts Association

This body was established in 2013, and by 2022, players were showcasing their talents at the World Matchplay finals on stage in Blackpool's Winter Gardens event. There are two categories: Classic – for players with upper and/or lower body impairments, or Paralympic conditions, or wheelchair users; and Compris – the inclusive division for all disabilities, and mental and/or physical impairments recognised by the UK government. There's also a World Team Cup, and more singles and team events being added regularly. The WDDA's slogan is 'Paralitas quod equitas' – fairness and equity.

World ParaDarts

An associate member of the World Darts Federation and a worldwide organisation, formed in 2020, World ParaDarts is working to try and get recognition by the International Paralympic Committee. To that end, they embrace the IPC's classification system, support all other disability darts organisations, promote the game and intend to provide a World ParaDarts Grand Slam of tournaments for international players. Now there are two classifications: World ParaDarts, which follow the Paralympic guidelines, and Inclusio ParaDarts, for all disabled players. www.worldparadarts.com

British Disability Darts Association

Established in 2016 with the involvement of Sarah Smale, who went on to sit on the World ParaDarts board, the BDDA works on IPC classification to ensure fair play and hosts its own ranking tournaments, which have the goal of qualifying for the BDDA Winmau Masters and World Championships. The association's first ambassador was the late Andy 'The Viking' Fordham. britishdisabilitydarts.co.uk

The innovator: Russ Strobel

Russ Strobel was responsible for recommending dartboards be hung at a 137cm-to-bull level, initially to Darts Australia. He worked it out by noting that the standard height of the board (173cm to bull) was based on the average height of an Englishman in 1920: 5ft 8ins. Russ simply mapped that onto the height said Englishman would be if using a wheelchair. Hence, 137cm. The exact sum was actually 136.5cm but that extra half a centimetre rounded up makes it easier to remember – 137/173. The length of the oche is the same, though both wheels must be behind the line. Strobel has even suggested a rotating board, on which one side is 137 and the other 173, to enable wheelchair users to compete against able-bodied darts players. Russ founded the World Disability Darts Association in 2012.

PLAY IT: TENNIS

GAME

Players:

Two or four (aka a doubles match)

In brief:

Win the set – or play the best of three/five sets.

How to play:

First, each player throws with their non-dominant hand (i.e. left, for right-handed darters, and vice versa): closest to the bull 'serves' first, becoming player one. If you're in teams, do the same – but the order of play always alternates. Therefore: team one, player one; team two, player one; team one, player two; team two, player two, in that order. Only the very closest dart counts to set up who goes first, and thereafter you must take it in turns. You'll need the scoreboard for this one.

The first 'service' game starts aiming *only* at the left-hand numbers on the board: this mirrors the way the real game of tennis changes sides to start each serve. The server can aim at any of the numbers on that side, and then that number becomes the active (scoring) number for that game. The server then accumulates as many points as they can on that number. So, if player one serves to 19, they can only score off 19.

The scoring system is as follows:

Single: 15 points
Two singles: 30 points
Three singles (or a treble): 40 points
Four singles (or a treble and a single): game won
Double (on first dart): ace – automatic win

The serving player has three darts in total, including the one that sets the active number. Note that this first dart is also a scoring dart in itself, so the server scores 15. After three darts, player/team two also aims at the active number (here, we've put 19 as an example), with the scoring as above – aside from an ace, which can only be scored on the first dart. Then player one/team one player two serves, and so on until someone wins the game.

Alternate between sides of the board (representing

the court) each time. So, player two can only aim at the right-hand side of the board on their turn.

Continue until somebody wins six games, and therefore the set. You may play on to the best of three or five sets in this manner. You may well end up with a score of 6–6; if so, a tiebreak game continues until one player or team wins by two points.

The left-hand numbers are 19, 7, 16, 8, 11, 14, 9, 12, 5.

The right-hand numbers are 17, 2, 15, 10, 6, 13, 4, 18, 1.

Hitting 20 or 3 once means a 'let' point and the server can throw again – with two darts in hand. Hitting either of these numbers twice on your serve is a double fault and gives the point to the opponent/s.

Variation one

Omit the three-darts rule and allow players to keep coming back to the board until they miss the target number. The player will either get to the winning total (i.e. hit the target a total of five times) or let in the opponents, who have at least three darts at it. Player/team two can similarly keep going until they either win the game or miss the active number.

Variation two

Two in a bed: once a number has been served and a point scored off it, it becomes inactive for the rest of the match. Therefore, if 19 is the first point, as in our example, it is added to the 'let point' numbers 20 and 3. The board/court thus gets smaller every game, making it much more challenging. Make sure you note which numbers are out of play on the board, 'cause there's no Hawk-Eye system or ball persons that look remarkably like Elton John on this one, folks. And watch out, of course, for that telltale chalk dust rising.

'It's like trying to pin down a kangaroo on a trampoline.'

'MY DARTING DAY' BY BRIAN 'NOT GONNA DIE' DARTSTONE

As a squillionaire entrepreneur, totally normal guy, longevity expert and man of the people I'm often asked: 'Brian, what the hell are you doing in my bedroom again? Get the hell out, you pervert.' Now as we both know, what people really mean by that is: 'How can I get to be exactly like you and live your wonderful life? I love you more than crisps.' And you can't blame them. I am very famous, and by the way, my skin is not transparent – that is a dirty lie by jealous cretins.

Here's an exclusive for you: aside from my expertise in taking untested Chinese research chemicals, measuring my night-time wees and drinking the blood of my sons, I'm also an accomplished dartister, having scored 180 many times when nobody was looking but I got a seven-darter once, I swear, and won the Intergalactic Championships, and you can't prove I didn't.

If you want to live forever like me, and learn the secret to the strange green glowing residue I leave on the floor wherever I've been, here's a snapshot of my daily regime.

2:30am – Wake up

For me, being awake helps me to do my routine. You might want to try it. As soon as the little Mickey hand goes to the number two and the big Mickey hand goes to the number six, my 'clock' (check Wikipedia) makes a special noise – and that noise means 'no more eepys for Dartstone!' *Righteous!*

2:45am – First prayer

Stay humble. I lie with my eyes closed in silent prayer, which sounds a bit like someone snoring, but that's just a Zen trick I learned from a sect of Scottish monks when I spent six years at a mountain retreat in the Highlands led by Master J. Wilson. It is in fact the sound of one dart clapping.

4:45am – Wake up

When Mickey's little hand has gone near to, but not onto, the number five, and his big hand is on the number nine, that special tune plays again! Time to stop praying and get out there to grab the world by the throat and choke it until it sputters out the good puke. *Boom!*

5:00am – Breakfast

In order to conquer the world of darts one must *become* the world of darts. Therefore, I munch down on a nutritious mixture of sawdust from an old dartboard, moistened by the sweat dripping from the roof at the world championship finals, Lakeside.

5:05am – Expellation

I spend some time in the toilet area as my stomach cleanses itself fully, expelling the unwanted residue of non-dartistry. But I never flush – this is powerful stuff so I collect it in bowls for later topping-up sips as I work out. Speaking of which . . .

6:00am – Workout

Ten reps of throwing-arm lifts, a hundred burps, six dummy receipts of a mock trophy, a hundred clenched fists. You might want to add a set of turning to your left and shouting *'fucking get in'* to an imaginary camera, to make sure it becomes muscle memory and second nature when you're in a real match.

8:00am – Shower

I grease up my perfect naked body with the finest blend of motor oil, mulch and any leftover expellations before standing in my floor-to-ceiling windows and dripping dry as the world goes by outside. I can tell by the looks of the public that they are shocked at my incredible physique and my utter commitment to darts perfection. Though the police are still as ignorant as ever and keep sending me summonses, which as a freeman of the land I ignore, of course.

9:00am – Silent prayer

I lie down once more to contemplate the magnificent game of darts, which again, let me stress, *can* sound almost exactly like someone snoring. *But it's not!*

1:00pm – Lunch

Six chocolate peanuts, which I lick all the chocolate off then spit the nuts out of the window, followed by a spoonful of Afghanistani Shilajit and a handful of pissy Chernobyl nettles (for the uranium content). Yum! The local cats love my peanut pile! (Or are they rats? No difference really, is there? Anyway, I have people to 'rehome' them. *Bang! Miaow! Silence!*)

1:15pm – Expellation

As some of this nutritious stuff has now been through my body twice it has become ultra-concentrated in its power. Again, I scoop it up from the bowl into one of them squirty bottles like what athletes have, so I can sip on it and look cool while I go about my day. *Whomp!*

1:30pm – Cryochamber

Tip: a real cryochamber is extremely expensive, so do what I do and go to the local park, get naked and lie fully immersed in the duck pond with only a little bamboo straw in my mouth so I can breathe underwater. *So cleansing!*

3:30pm – Supplements and medication

Taken on a cycle, so don't fall off: Megafool 3mg x2; Pla-C-Bo 10mg x4; Cornholio TP 300mg (powder); TWA Tea 2 sachets; X.PensiveBolox 4 scoops; Lytteral-Shyte 1000mg (orange); Du B-Os supplement 4oz mix; Garlic 5 cloves; dihydrogen monoxide – 1 cup; Sawyer Cumin 333mg; CyaNexTues 1.2–1.5; C12H22011 3000mg; Extended NaCl (McD brand) 500g; and finally, a good old bracing insufflation of C10H15N, a special 'pick-me-up' formula that my nutritionist guru MathHead[1] recommended to me last time I met him around the back of the Dalek & Rasta. Warning: *it's pretty moreish!*

4:00pm (day one) to 8:00am (day two) – dancing and meditation

Take this time to relax once more, through the fine art of interpretive dance (which looks a *bit* like twitching and running around the room very fast but I can assure you is *not*).

8:00am – Ring Guru MathHead to acquire re-dose

Brian's Top Tip: repeat every five minutes until he replies. He may let out noises akin to someone swearing, as he expels the negativity out of his body, but after the promise of triple payment, he will come and meet me as he usually does. I wait in my Alone Room, getting

1 I think that's his name? I've heard people call him something like this, though I've never asked him how to spell it. He must be good at sums, because everyone tells me if I want to score good Math then he's the guy. He doesn't like me calling it 'math' though, 'specially if there's people about. He prefers 'ice' or 'glass'. Strange fellow. Kinda nervy.

to know myself more and inhaling from my ignited Herbal Health Spice Sticks, which MathHead highly recommends for this part of the day.

10:00am – Talk with MathHead

The Guru is a man of few words but as I am a billionaire crypto magician I can always persuade him to spend some time chewing the fat about the ins and outs of how strong I am and how strong I feel and how amazing the C10 is today and does he want to go and *eff some ess up* (my way of speaking at his 'level' – it means 'playing darts'!). Because he knows I am superior at the game he always demurs unless I 'persuade' him with some more paper money. (This 'cash' is destined to be useless in the future! He knows nothing!) MathHead usually leaves at 11:00am at the latest because he has to pick up his kids from school – even on a Sunday! They're so committed to learning – perhaps I could learn from them! (I couldn't – they're idiots.)

Midday–8:00pm – Self-knowledge

Watching inspirational workout videos – those muscular men are very supportive of each other. If only I had a partner to do these intimate reps with, it would be a boon.

Brian's Top Tip: Keep some oil handy in case of friction burns! And switch hands occasionally.

8:30pm – Plasma infusion

I puncture my son's arm and drink heavily from the nectar inside. Such fun! Sometimes I playfully throw him into the sea, *as a joke!!* It only makes him laugh (scream) harder. Often the police fail to understand but it seems that's their job. Bunch of sourpusses! (I can always see them coming anyway so I have a special hidey-hole but I'm not telling you where it is, and it's definitely not behind that fake bookshelf in the nook next to the drawing room.) *Agadoo!*

9:00pm – Practise darts

It's time to lie down in my room again and think about all the amazing darts I will be playing tomorrow. Remember – do not over-practice! I visualise winning the World Championships. Soon I am tuckered out so I drop off – that's as long as the radioactive muscle spiders aren't crawling all over me and coming at me in the dark. Oh, God – please, not again. Please! MathHead says it's just natural, though.

2:30am – Wake up

The amazing process starts all over again – it may seem a tough regime, but I can tell you it's not easy being a multi-billionaire who will live forever. Remember – Not Gonna Die by nickname, Not Gonna Die by name! Unless I have to go to the emergency ward again, which can happen occasionally (about three times a week).[2] As the world-famous saying goes: Now let us do a game of darting! *Wazzical! Boof it good!*

2 Publishers' note: Sadly, Brian Dartstone disappeared completely shortly after this book was published. As yet we have heard nothing more from him, but as he gave us a big wad of what he called 'outdated paper so-called money' we're legally bound to print this. Do not do any of this stuff at home, or at all, obviously. Mind how you go.

DARTS IN THE CHARTS

Bros and Dexys have the main claims to fame in many ways when it comes to darts, but over the years there've been quite a few musicians who have paid tribute to the glorious game. Here's a few of our favourite artists and some songs that are related in some way to the darts. Which ones have we missed?

Bands

Band: Darts
Genre: Doo-wop-rock-pop
From: London, UK
About: A nine-piece 1950s revival pop-and-rock outfit which found fame from the mid-1970s to the mid-1980s. Produced at one stage by Tommy Boyce, who'd done a similar job for popular boy band/Beatles knock-offs The Monkees in the 1960s.
Hits: 'Duke of Earl' (produced by Roy Wood); 'Daddy Cool'/'The Girl Can't Help It' (medley); 'The Boy From New York City'
Trivia: Singer Den Hegarty left in 1978 to go solo and

ended up hosting TV shows including crazed Saturday morning madness *Tiswas*. In the 2010s he was a psychology lecturer at Exeter College!

Band: The Darts
Genre: Punk/garage-rock
From: Seattle, USA
About: All-female noisy punk brilliance. The quartet was signed to venerable punk label Alternative Tentacles by one-time Dead Kennedys frontman Jello Biafra. The band has toured with such names as The Longshot (featuring Billie Joe Armstrong of Green Day). A wild, high-octane ferocious onstage presence melds with smouldering spookiness to create a blend of Stooges chaos and pure rock energy.
Hits: None to speak of in the traditional sense but check out the self-titled LP, or the Biafra-produced *Snake Oil* to get the full picture.
Trivia: Featured on the soundtrack on the TV super-hit *Peaky Blinders*.

Band: The Arrows
Genre: Pop/glam rock
From: London, UK

About: Four-piece outfit managed by Peter Meaden, who was the boss of The Who in the first years of the 1960s. Most notable for securing two, 14-week-long television series on Granada TV in 1976 and 1977. Recorded 'I Love Rock 'n' Roll' by Arrows vocalist/ bassist Alan Merrill – that track was later covered to huge success first by Joan Jett & the Blackhearts and then, slightly bizarrely, Britney Spears.
Hits: 'I Love Rock 'n' Roll'; 'Touch Too Much' (not the AC/DC song); 'Toughen Up'
Trivia: 'Movin' Next Door To You' has been used on the soundtrack of *Homes Under the Hammer* on BBC TV.

Songs

Song: 'Theme From *Shaft*'
Genre: Funk
Artist: Isaac Hayes
About: One of the coolest songs of all time, from one of the coolest soundtracks of all time, from one of the coolest movies of all time, sung by one of the coolest mofos of all time. What more can we say?
Trivia: Isaac Hayes won two Grammys in 1972 for the soundtrack to the movie *Shaft*, and the 1971 recording

of this awesome track is now in the Grammy Hall of Fame.

Song: 'Flight of Icarus'
Genre: Heavy metal
Band: Iron Maiden
About: Heavy metal, and Maiden specifically, at their chugging, epic storytelling best on this track from 1983's *Piece of Mind.* Features an absolutely masterful vocal from silly-trousered singer Bruce Dickinson, including the world's best ever 'mm-hmm' on record. Wonderful, daft, irresistible stuff.
Trivia: Reached No. 11 in the UK and No. 8 in the States on its April, 1983 release. And, OK, it's about the Icarus myth not his darts, but what a song – and that final note by Dicko is incredible.

Song: 'On a Ragga Tip'
Genre: Happy hardcore/breakbeat
Band: SL2
About: Reggae skankin' that will take the older generation right back to long nights in fields in the middle of nowhere, waving neon glowsticks around and sharing bottled water with strangers before it all went

wrong and they ended up half-naked in the morning light surrounded by weirdos and police. Well, it was good while it lasted. Released in April 1992, it's music for the Prodigy/*Jilted Generation* crowd.

Trivia: Samples 'Walk and Skank' by Jah Screechy toasting out some words of English mixed with Jamaican patois. Nobody ever really knew what it all meant or indeed what the hell was going on – standard for the time really.

TV shows

TV Show: *Pointless*

Genre: Quiz

About: Pairs of contestants have to pick the least popular answer from questions previously asked to 100 people, in a kind of reverse *Family Fortunes* affair. Watching over proceedings are exceedingly posh Alexander Armstrong and various celeb guest-hosts to replace original co-presenter Richard Osman. Oh, and the prize money's absolutely crap usually – unless it's built up un-won for several days.

Trivia: As the title might suggest, there's not a lot of darts content (no point, literally). However, Osman did once play against Phil 'The Power' Taylor on a charity edition of the show. He scored a dreadful 22 (though he also had a head start of 100), which Taylor easily beat with a nonchalant 38, practically with his eyes closed. Darts fan Richard Osman has also played the game in events for Comic Relief.

'He's as happy as a hound-dog who's won a year's supply of Boneo.'

'His face is sagging with tension.'

DARTS LEGEND

Name: Robert Francis 'Bobby' George

Nickname: The King of Darts / Bobby Dazzler / Mr Glitter

Date of birth: 16th December, 1945

Place of birth: Manor Park, London, England

Active since: 1976

Darts: 23g Winmau Bobby George (Right-Handed)

Walk-on music: Queen: 'We Are the Champions'

Shirt: Bling, bling, bling in many colours

Notable achievements: Former builder; double *News of the World* champion; twice runner-up in WDF finals; semi-finalist in World Masters; winner of Europe Cup singles and team events with WDF (1982); lost 1994 World Championship 6–0 to John Part but later revealed he was playing with a broken back that required eight screws in his spine; walk-ons got more and more elaborate and included candelabras, crowns, robes and much kingly bling, so hugely influential sartorially; many TV appearances in comedies, darts-related shows, dance shows, *The Real Marigold Hotel* (2016); son Richie is a former pro who once reached the semis of BDO's World Darts Championship; ambassador for mathematics, touring schools to show how darts can assist with arithmetic; has raised a million pounds for charity; claimed in a book that he'd once beaten the Canadian arm-wrestling champion.

Controversies: Caused a stir by saying Phil 'The Power' Taylor in his heyday couldn't compete with Luke Littler (Chris Mason called it 'bollocks' almost immediately); rather than join the fledgling PDC in 1994, he stayed with the BDO – though he said basically that nobody had asked him to switch; used to go around various pubs in his early career alongside Eric Bristow trying to win cash from the locals; sadly, Bobby's pub in his former mansion George Hall had to close down; not impressed by a proposed ban on walk-on models, saying that he married one in his long-time wife Marie; said in his book, *Bobby Dazzler*, that as a kid, he once knocked out one of his teachers in the boxing ring.

Quote: 'Scoring for show, doubles for dough' – though this has been attributed to many, many people.

'It's the nearest thing to public execution this side of Saudi Arabia.'

'He's perspiring like a pudding in a pot.'

QUIZ

DARTS ON SCREEN AND IN FICTION

Our wonderful game is so captivating that plenty of fiction has been written about it, and while we're used to seeing characters have a game or two down the Rovers Return on *Coronation Street*, actual darts movies are few and far between. That fact alone is going to make this quiz one of the more difficult ones in this book – or is it? Let's see how far the small and big screens – and those fancy wads of paper alike – have permeated the cultural darting conversation . . .

1. Books, first: this novel, by a famous English author, is the tale of a writer with a terminal illness. One of the other key characters is an extremely dodgy wannabe pro dartist by the name of Keith Talent. For a point each, name the author and the 1989 novel.

2. The saintly Welsh wonderman Michael Sheen plays Colin in this under-the-radar 2003 movie. Colin runs a news agency and his wife Sandra plays darts with a team in the Athletic Arms. Adultery, team chaos and love rivalries ensue. What's the name of the film?

a. *Homelander*
b. *Heartbeat*
c. *Heartlands*

3. Katy Brand plays Big Sheila in this one, opposite Jonny Owen as Andy 'The Arrows' Samson. Released in 2009, it was written by Irvine Welsh. Name the film.

a. *Game Shot*
b. *Good Arrows*
c. *Double Top*

4. And what heroin-gnarly movie is Welsh arguably most famous for?

a. *Flatliners*
b. *Trainspotting*
c. *Skag on Tour*

5. Staying with the same movie, there is a scene in Alex (Jenny Agutter)'s flat, where darts is on telly. Name the two players.

a. Rab Smith and Cliff Lazarenko
b. Eric Bristow and Jocky Wilson
c. Adrian Lewis and Ron Craggs

6. We're going to watch this one tonight: it's about a son who somehow has to save his mam's eyesight by drinking lots of beer and playing darts. We'll need subtitles for this mad-arse movie, though, 'cause the 2021 Amazon Prime video is originally in German. What do we reckon it's called?

a. *Das Dartist*
b. *Heiko's Welt*
c. *Schoenberg 180*

7. Why is the darts player in *An American Werewolf in London* angry with the character called Jack?

a. Jack has brought in the cold and not shut the door
b. Jack wants to play pool instead
c. Jack has made him miss the board for the first time ever

8. Tough one here: what's the name of the actor that plays said darts player?

a. David Hemp
b. David Schofield
c. David Duke

9. A fictional documentary from 2022 now, courtesy of Simon Sprackling. Rocky Goldfingers is the flash darts player played by Geoff Ball – and he's in prison for murdering a rival. He says he's innocent, naturally. Enough spoilers – what's this excellent fly-on-the-wall type piece of cockney crime comedy drama called?

a. *Poison Arrows*
b. *The Looks of Love*
c. *Tears Are Not Enough*

10. In a fabulous scene in the wonderful TV series *Ted Lasso*, the titular character plays the nasty pasty Rupert in a game of darts. Rupert expects to blow him away, but Ted quietly wins with style, showing that he's not to be underestimated. What's the name of the actor and comedian who also created *Ted Lasso*?

a. Jason Lee
b. Jason Bourne
c. Jason Sudeikis

'As Freud said to Jung in Vienna, you can psych up too much for a darts match.'

PLAY IT: BASEBALL

GAME

Also known as:

Baseball darts

> You can buy (or make) a designated (outdoor) Dartball dartboard with entirely different rules, throwing style and leagues, particularly in the States – but here we're concentrating on the standard dartboard version, playable indoors from standard distance.

Players:

No no, no no no no, no no no no, no no, there's no limit

In brief:

Score the most runs over nine innings.

How to play:

Simpler than it seems: use the numbers 1 to 9, in order, for each 'innings' (visit). Each player has their own column on the scoreboard. So, for innings one, everyone will be throwing at 1; innings five, everyone trying to score from 5, and so on up to ninth innings and 9 being the scoring number. Hit a single, and score one run. Hit a double, it's two runs, and obviously the treble is three runs. Note that these scores persist over all targets rather than adding up the total amount, so a treble 4 is still 3 points (not 12, as in 501). This means you can technically score nine points on each innings (i.e. three trebles) so the scores could get pretty high.

Each player has a visit per innings, then the game moves to the next innings. Highest cumulative score at the bottom of the ninth is the winner. If, at the bottom (i.e. the end) of the ninth, there is a drawn game, those players go on to a tenth innings, aiming at 10. Continue with these extra innings until someone wins, including bull. If it's still a draw after bull, you're gonna have to think of a way to end the game before everyone gets really old and starts popping their clogs. Maybe handicap people by giving them access to unlimited hot dogs or massive glasses of root beer and sarsaparilla, whatever the hell that is.

Variation one

Get a famous actor, singer or celebrity to throw the first pitch of the innings (i.e. chuck a dart at the board to get it all under way). You may have to improvise here and do an impression of Taylor Swift or something. Extra points for coming dressed as Tay-Tay, which'd probably be absolutely fine in Frimley Green (but might get you a few odd looks down the Dog & Drongo on a Saturday night).

Variation two

Rather than a series of individuals playing each innings, create two teams – players take an innings each, then start again from player one of the team. To make sure everyone gets a fair turn, extend (or reduce) the game until everyone's had the same amount of visits. So, a three-player team game is still nine innings; a two- or four-player team game could be eight or 12; a six-player team game can be six or 12 depending on how much time you've got. Seven-, eight- and nine-player teams stick to the same amount of innings as the number of players. You can always have a rematch straight away – the baseball season is about 150 games long and they play day in, day out, so you'll be on point with the original this way.

Variation three

Halve-it halfway through: if someone completely misses with all their darts in, say, the fifth innings, their accumulated score is cut in half. Annoying, but certainly piles on the pressure as the game continues.

Variation four

Handicap: a mixed-ability team or game can level the playing field somewhat by making the better players only score from doubles or trebles (or both). This does mean that the really skilful dartists will look to accumulate much bigger scores, so you could also be completely fiendish and specify that, for the better players, doubles and/or trebles *only count as a single point.* Similarly, you could specify that the fifth innings is a double-up innings and any runs scored during that innings count double (singles = 2; doubles = 4; trebles = 6).

WHAT'S YOUR POISON? WHAT YOUR CHOICE OF DRINK AT THE DARTS SAYS ABOUT YOU . . .

Science! What a thing it is. All mathsy and graphs and experiments and whatnot. We love it. In fact, we love science so much that we've asked some Top Scientist People to contribute to this very book. Yes, for the first time, we present the absolute definitive guide to what your darts drink says about you. Remember, what follows isn't our mere opinion – perish the thought! It's all been carefully calibrated from the responses of the world's top boffins, taking a moment from CERNing about, with all test tubes bubbling and neon liquids making smoke in beakers all over the place. #FACT. All drinks here work both for alcoholic and non-alcoholic versions, 'cause it's about style, damnit.

Drink: gin and tonic

What it means: You are steady as they come. A G&T is instantly recognisable and pretty difficult to mess up in any pub. It means you're not messing about with any fancy-ass beverages; you know what you like and you don't want any deviation. Another way to describe this is 'boring', but as we're a positive bunch we'll refrain.

Drink: lager

What it means: You're out on the piss and don't want to get too wrecked too quickly (in theory). Whether in pints or in poxy bottles with lime in the end like a total divvy's drink, lager is cold, thirst-quenching and relatively cheap. You'll probably end up with several pints' worth soaking into your James Brown fancy dress by the end of the evening, where it'll be joined by grease and chilli sauce from the kebab you guzzle on your way back to your digs.

Drink: red wine

What it means: You are over 35 and leaning into it. Why not get a bowl of olives and so on to go with it? You drive an Audi A4 with tinted windows and have thought about working as an estate agent 'cause the commissions are getting more and more attractive as the years go by. You've got a man cave.

Drink: JD & Coke

What it means: You listen to Motörhead and are prone to going on weekend adventures to Donington Park to watch what used to be called Monsters of Rock. Secretly, you'd rather have a pint of Old Fartybum's Dark Skies, but you've spent years cultivating your dangerous reputation so have to stick with it. You'd love a Harley-Davidson but never got around to actually learning to ride.

Drink: Jägerbombs

What it means: You've completely overestimated your ability to handle your drink and will be face down under the table by 2:26pm.

Drink: anything neon

What it means: You are on a stag/hen do and almost certainly dressed in a wedding frock with L-plates on it, particularly if you're a bloke. You will be drinking out of a bendy straw that has several loop-the-loops in it and wearing deely boppers that light up when you push a button. Your darts hero is Peter Wright, but you've stopped drinking snakebites after overdoing it at age 14 down the park swings, and you can't think about that without feeling nauseous again.

Drink: Newcy Brown

What it means: You're almost certainly from the Toon, 'cause nobody outside Newcastle ever drinks it except once in a while to jog their memory that it's a weirdly sweet and rather strange beverage that reminds you of real beer but is not quite the same. At the darts you'll be drinking it out of plastic glasses, too, which takes away even the mini-thrill of an ice-cold bottle where you can put your thumb over the blue star and make it go white as it heats up. (Or is it the other way around? We're not buying a bottle just to check, soz.)

Drink: Long Island iced tea

What it means: Essentially this is what is otherwise called a 'top shelf', which involves pouring any old crap into the same glass as long as it's from a spirits bottle. The Long Island iced tea can have vodka, rum, gin, tequila and possibly whisky in it – with a tiny splash of coke and some minging sweet triple sec to take the edge off. This is the drink of great regrets and blackouts, to the extent that not only will you not remember who won the title, you'll be unsure as to whether you actually attended the darts at all.

Drink: martini, shaken not stirred

What it means: You've come to the venue dressed in tails like James Bond, haven't you? And after you've had a martini or two you'll hoy the idea into the long grass and revert to a pint of Guinness instead. Let's be realistic: that bow tie will end up tied around your head like Rambo by the end of the night. Even more so if your choice of drink is an espresso martini – you'll be climbing the walls and talking thirteen-to-the-dozen about scoring averages over the league season. Nobody else will be listening, because you're speaking incredibly fast and twitching at the same time.

Drink: water

What it means: You're a superb person who doesn't care what anyone else thinks and you're there to have fun. Getting sozzled is something you do if you feel like it, but you never feel obliged just 'cause everyone else seems to be. You're a modern-day hero in many ways. Kudos to you, brave soldier.

Drink: aged single-malt whisky

What it means: You're a connoisseur of the finer things in life (or want people to think you are). You'll also bore everybody stupid with your explanation of how a single drop of water in the whisky 'opens up the flavours', and you'll do that thing where you swill it around in your glass and stare at it to see the 'legs'. You should be in a dusty old library somewhere, sitting in an ancient leather armchair near a blazing open fire, recounting stories that are borderline incomprehensible and end up with the words, 'I must admit that I was very, very drunk.'

Drink: nice cup of tea

What it means: You're hungover. Get it down ya, and start again.

'The fans now, with their eyes pierced on the dartboard.'

'OOOH, YOU'VE GOT ME POPPIN' . . .' ADRIAN LEWIS VS. BOB MORTIMER

Bob Mortimer is, these days, a bona fide National Treasure. He's come a long way from his first stage work alongside the similarly revered Vic Reeves in the latter's left-field, surreal comedy stylings as *Big Night Out*. That duo soon moved from the back rooms of London pubs – Bob ditching his career as a solicitor along the way – to TV fame and decades of huge telly hits. *Big Night Out* led to (among many other weird and wonderful shows) the splendid quiz show *Shooting Stars,* via *Catterick,* plus a remake of *Randall and Hopkirk (Deceased)*, and for Bob, a late-career piece of loveliness alongside old mate Paul Whitehouse in the superbly bucolic *Gone Fishing*.

Mortimer is a long-standing/long-suffering fan of Middlesbrough FC, his hometown team – but Reeves' interest in footy is famously absent. Hence why dear old Bob, convalescing from a heart op, began for the first time in his career a project based on the Beautiful Game. He roped in journalist Andy Dawson (a Sunderland lad) along the way, and the result is the very daft, very inventive podcast *Athletico Mince*. Inevitably, *Mince* soon veered off the soccer rails, driven by Mortimer's inimitable brain and Dawson's reliably eager support and own ideas, becoming a frazzly-round-the-edges sketch show involving everything from Jeremy Corbyn's constant one-upmanship (one of Andy's), through Mortimer's liaisons with the local Alderman (always ending in kissing), tales of a remote Scottish island (Bob again) and the life of Peter Beardsley (Bob's impression is spot on).

It's hard enough to describe *Athletico Mince* so please do yourself a favour and just listen to it. At the very least it's two mates talking absolute nonsense that's vaguely about footy – and when those mates happen to be so unbelievably entertaining, you've got a total winner on your hands.

But what does this have to do with darts? Well, nothing, and everything. Bob and Andy both often introduce new bits, the anarchic set-up being perfect to try out something half-thought-out and explore its bizarro world just for the sake of it. One of Mortimer's self-admitted pastimes is watching telly, particularly sport, and particularly the darts – which Dawson also absolutely loves.

It was equally inevitable, then, that Mortimer would bring in a sketch on that theme. Specifically, that Bob claimed to have seen Adrian Lewis, the hugely talented darts player, go into a restaurant near the Alexandra Palace sports venue in North London. Moreover, that restaurant revels in the name of Slaughters. Intrigued, Mortimer follows Lewis inside the meat-only eatery and records the darts player as he is taken through a menu of growing meaty disgustingness. Lewis drinks meat juices, dripping or gravy; he eats lard, trotters, hen's kidneys, things rammed into seals, carcasses; he has a massive dog; he is always served by an aggressively swearing, sarcastic waiter; eventually we meet the chef, Ron Craggs, who is likely to storm the restaurant with a massive cleaver if a punter's talking out of turn. As the episodes continue, the sketches get more and more sweary, more and more full of weird things to do with dead animals, and 'Adrian' calls Craggs/the waiter 'a meaty genius' – while sweating buckets in anticipation of his feast. Special guests also feature – Steve McClaren and his pet snake Casper and Peter 'Snakebite' Wright among them – as the sketches get weirder and weirder.

Now, at this point, it's important to note that this

is all *entirely* a figment of the comedian's vivid and extremely strange imagination . . . we think. You can watch animations of some of the sketches online, too, courtesy of BenPics.

As for Adrian himself – well, despite being rather bemused (and who wouldn't be?), he takes it all in good spirit. After all, there's not many world-class darts players who have a world-class comedian writing sketches about them. The double darts world champion Jackpot Lewis has also been spotted enjoying a day or two of fishing, so who knows what might come next in this most offbeat of sports/podcast mashups? Oooooh . . .

'He's got one foot in the frying pan and one on thin ice.'

THAT AIN'T DARTS, BUT WE'LL GIVE IT A GO

Basically, people have wanted to chuck/aim/shoot stuff at targets for thousands of years. We've got the wonderful game of modern darts to keep us on the straight and arrow, but have you ever considered trying your prowess at any of the below? As ever, be safe and only try these sports in the company of licensed professionals, 'cause we're really not keen on doing any paperwork if anyone ends up Harold-ing their mate's eye out, OK?

Archery

The big kahuna. The one that is perhaps the most familiar to any darts player.

How to play:

Shoot an arrow from a bow at a board and get closest to the centre to score the most points.

Background

Skill with a bow has been prized for many, many thousands of years across the globe. The basic technology is a high-tensile string suspended on a semi-rigid, semi-circular bow. This creates, effectively, a pair of cantilever springs (thanks, Wikipedia), which stores elastic energy. Your arrow is a straight stick with a pointy end and some feathers at the other to help it fly straight. Place the pointy end at the bow, and the feathery end in the hand that holds the tensed bowstring. Aim, and let go. Simple to describe, harder to control. The bow and arrow has been a hunting (and war) tool for so long that the oldest arrowheads are from around 50,000 years ago. That's almost as old as your mum.

Play it

Plenty of clubs around – and it's an Olympic sport so you can really go very far if you're any cop.

Axe-throwing

Unleash your inner Viking by hurling a massive sharp axe at a wall. You big butch beast.

How to play:

Chuck an axe at a target to score points.

Background

As with archery, axe-throwing has been a feature of war

and hunting for millennia. Native Americans are often cited as an example, as are the Franks on this side of the pond. People who have legitimate reasons to own sharp axes – woodsmen, lumberjacks and whatnot – have long tested their accuracy in contests. The Global Axe Throwing Commission (not an indie band) generally used double-bladed axes for their contests. Gradually, clubs were formed all over the world, with axes and tomahawks used to aim at targets often cleft from tree trunks.

Play it

Festivals and the Backyard Axe Throwing League's events brought the sport into a more mainstream arena and you can even find indoor axe-throwing venues in sports complexes/fashionable bars these days, believe it or not. Try the World Axe Throwing League, Eurothrowers, or the National Axe Throwing Federation for more info. Beard-growing is optional.

Knife-throwing

Lob yer knives at a target. If you're completely insane, become a magician's assistant and have them chucked around you as you spin round in circles on a board.

How to play:

Throw knives at a target to score points.

Background

As anyone who's ever watched a decent spaghetti western knows, a knife-thrower is a dangerous person; the weapon is small enough to carry in one hand, but sharp enough to be deadly. (It goes without saying that we absolutely condemn any carrying of knives as weapons.) As a sport, however, it's fascinating for its pinpoint accuracy (literally); the way the knives rotate in flight means that technique is as important as brute force, if not more so. The sport is very popular and involves targets similar to those used for archery. There's a World Knife Throwing League, which pretty much does what it says on the tin. Not bad for a sport first seen at circuses in the US and Europe, or in Far Eastern martial arts and African hunting demonstrations.

Play it

A dangerous one, this, so be sure to check that a club is indeed overseen by WKTL or an equivalently suitable governing body.

Shooting

Like darts, but with a gun, and boards that last about half a minute. Popular with Americans, where they like to practise it *al fresco* with unwitting targets.

Disc golf

Chuck a Frisbee into a kind of bucket from a designated tee. Yes, this really exists.

How to play:

Over 9 or 18 holes, throw the disc from the tee into the hole in as few throws as possible, playing your next throw from where the previous one landed.

Background

Probably invented by students in 1960s America, Frisbee golf has developed since then and now has its own Professional Disc Golf Association, loads of designated courses and players all over the world. The vast majority – three-quarters – are from the USA, though. The PDGA now has rules for competitive play. As with golf, there are different discs for chucking far (the equivalent of drivers), and more accurate, slower ones for 'putting' as you near the actual hole (a basket on a stick, with chain link around it).

Play it

All you need is a target and a Frisbee, really, and you can make up your own game. The PDGA run various tourneys and you can become a member as you see fit. And you will get fit with all that throwing, walking and arguing about whose disc that really is stuck up in the tree.

Javelin

Get an enormous, single dart and absolutely launch the fuggin' thing as far as you can.

How to play:

Get a javelin and chuck it. Preferably in a designated track-and-field centre, with coaches and safety-type stuff.

Background

As a competitive sport it was first seen at the Ancient Olympics in 708BCE, which is when your mum was only about 10 years old. It originally had two disciplines: the familiar distance throwing contest, and one in which you had to hit a target for accuracy, which gives us the link to darts. The modern javelin was reintroduced as a popular sport in the late 1880s by target-keen throwers in Scandinavia and Germany, from where the distance event was reintegrated for the modern Olympics a decade or two later.

Play it

Head to your local sports centre for advice on how to get into this excellent sport. If javelin ain't your bag, you might be better suited to other throwing sports including hammer, discus or shot-put, which are all excellent names for *Gladiators*.

Ski-jump javelin darts

A modern combination of several popular sports.

How to play:

Get dressed up for a ski jump, and go to the top of the ski jump. Take a javelin with you. When you zoom down to the end of the jump and just as you launch into space, chuck the javelin as best you can into an enormous dartboard suspended high in the air, 30 metres off the ground and 30 metres away. Each player has three jumps per visit, and the aim is to get from 501 to 0 as quickly as possible, ending on a double.

Background

We just made it up.

Play it

If anyone ever *does* manage to get this set up, please film it and send it to us. We reckon it's defo gonna be our *Dragons' Den* pitch. What do you mean, 'Ah'm oot'??

'They're sweating like a pair of giraffes coming up to a mirage water hole.'

'He's playing out of his pie crust.'

PLAY IT: BERMUDA TRIANGLE

GAME

Also known as:

Halve-it

Players:

One or more.

In brief:

Score points from a series of designated numbers and avoid having to cut your score in half.

How to play:

Each round has a different active number that players must hit. Doubles and trebles are also in play. Keep a track of each player's scores on the scoreboard. The game lasts for 13 rounds and many people play as follows:

Round	Target
1	12
2	13
3	14
4	Any double
5	15
6	16
7	17
8	Any treble
9	18
10	19
11	20
12	Both inner and outer bull, but both only score 25
13	Only the inner bull, scoring 50

Tiebreak

An additional round with the target being 11, and going down by one target number until someone scores more points than the opponent – therefore winning.

For example, player one hits single 12 and double 12 (24), scoring a total of 36 points. Player two hits single 12, so scores 12 on round one. The game then moves on to 13 as round two. However, in their second-round visit, player one misses 13 entirely. As a result, their total score is halved, so they are now on 18 points. Continue until round 13 has been completed, and the highest total final score wins. Note that as the rounds reach the final stages the scores increase considerably – and should you miss your target in your three-darts visit, the more points you've accumulated then the more you will lose. Think strategically: the early rounds have less jeopardy in terms of going for the doubles and trebles, though you might want to keep it tight throughout and be a Steady Eddie all the way through. Keep an eye on that accumulating score!

Variation one

Make it trickier by only using the area between trebles and bull – that is, only single numbers count but the board is considerably smaller. Great for your aim. Similarly, you can make only doubles and trebles active, eliminating the single beds completely: this is pretty fiendish and if you're going to go into minus scores then carnage will follow.

Variation two

Nominate any numbers on the board for the rounds, as above. The scores will be lower, but the advantage here is to learn the board extremely well as a result. Set up the rounds based on 16/8/4/2/1 and 20/10/5 and work on your finishes.

Variation three

Minimum score: this truly is a bugger of a variation, but as it's the same for everyone it works best if you're all around the same level of skill. For example, set a minimum score of 20 for all rounds: this means in effect that aside from round 11, you're going to have to either get multiple singles on your visit to each number, or hit a multiplier double/treble. Either way, it's a toughie.

Variation four

Rather than using designated beds for each round, decide on a minimum score. So, round one must be a score of, say, 20 or more – using any part of the board. Up the score each round by 5 points each time, so on round two each player must exceed 25, on round three it's 30, etc. If a player doesn't hit the score in three darts, their score is halved. End on the bull as above. You could also designate a finishing double if you wished.

'I don't know what he's had for breakfast but Taylor knocked the snap, crackle and pop outta Bristow.'

'There was less noise when Pompeii was swamped in lava.'

QUIZ

WALK ON, WALK ON

Walk-on music is absolutely key to setting the scene for any darts player. Not only does it ramp up the tension, it can also reflect heritage, attitude, nickname, background and your own music tastes. Nowhere else aside from boxing has such a body-shaking introduction to players and it's proved so popular that they even try to do it in the snooker these days. Let's take a look at some walk-on songs and see whether you're more of a Dimitri or a Snakebite: simply choose your answers and tot up how many of a, b or c you've accumulated. We'll let you know what that means at the end. More Hot and Sweaty Science, folks.

Note that this can also be played as a quiz: simply name the player whose walk-on music we've noted here. Answers in the back, of course. And, yes, we're fully aware that those awkward buggers might change their walk-on music just as we go to print . . .

1. Which one of these songs sums you up best?
a. Kaiser Chiefs: 'I Predict a Riot'
b. Elton John: 'I'm Still Standing'
c. David Guetta featuring Ne-Yo: 'Play Hard'

2. If you were at the World Championships, which one of these would you choose to get the crowd on your side?
a. The White Stripes: 'Seven Nation Army'
b. Billy Ocean: 'Red Light Spells Danger'
c. Walk The Moon: 'Shut Up and Dance'

3. And to psyche out your opponent?
a. Black Sabbath: 'Paranoid'
b. Vic Reeves and the Wonder Stuff: 'Dizzy'
c. Pitbull featuring TJR: 'Don't Stop the Party'

4. Which one would get your juices flowing as you made your way up to the oche?

a. House of Pain: 'Jump Around'
b. The Killers: 'Mr. Brightside'
c. Green Light featuring Flo Rida: 'Green Light'

5. Which one would the crowd be most likely to roar back at you?

a. Scooter: 'J'adore Hardcore'
b. Oasis: 'Don't Look Back in Anger'
c. Bob Marley and the Wailers: 'Three Little Birds'

If you scored . . .

Mostly As: *You're a rocker, a dangerous opponent who's gonna fight and scrape when your back's against the wall. The distortion and the driving beats resonate in your warrior heart. You're gonna get overexcited and get knocked out in round two for trying to get three nine-darters in a row.*

Mostly Bs: *You ain't going anywhere soon, but you have no regrets. You play every game as if it's your last, but you're not fazed by anything 'cause you've seen it all before. You're a veteran of the scene and keep coming back for your fix – whatever the results of your last shot at the competition.*

Mostly Cs: *Raver, lover, player. You're in it for the razzmatazz and the fireworks, and the first to get to the after-party. Your darts have 3D holograms of naked ladies on them. You dye your hair the same colour as your dodgy harem pants. You will wake up in Ibiza on a beach with no memory of how you got there.*

Which songs would you use?

How to play: each person involved in the game has a sheet of paper on which they write a song they reckon sums them up (get someone to type and print them if handwriting's obvious). Put them all into a hat. Pick one out, and try and guess who reckons their walk-on song should be 'Too Sick To Pray' by Alabama 3. In reality, it should be 'The Thrills Have Gone' by Alabama 3, and we all know it.

DARTS LEGEND

Name: Philip Douglas Taylor

Nickname: The Power

Date of birth: 13th August, 1960

Place of birth: Stoke-on-Trent, UK

Active since: 1987

Darts: 26g Target Signature Gen 11 (Right-Handed)

Walk-on music: Snap: 'The Power'

Shirt: Usually quite plain; in later years with The Power emblazoned on the rear.

Notable achievements: Arguably the greatest player of all time; was lent a significant sum by mentor Eric Bristow to go professional; promptly beat Bristow in the 1990 BDO World Darts Championship Final 6–1 as a 125/1 rank outsider; 214 professional tournament wins;

87 major titles; 16 World Championships including eight in a row; reached 14 consecutive World Championship finals; 11 televised nine-darters and 22 in total; first player to hit two nine-darters in the same match; six-time PDC player of the year; twice nominated for BBC Sports Personality of the Year (2006, and runner-up in 2010); retired in 2018 as runner-up in the World Championships; briefly competed in the World Senior Championships; retired in 2024.

Controversies: Found guilty in 2001 of indecently assaulting two women in his motorhome after a drinking competition in 1999 (he denied the assaults); failed in an injunction against a downmarket tabloid when the paper wanted to publish an interview with his daughters in 2015 following his split with their mother; embroiled in a strange 'cheating' accusation in 2013 after one of his darts was said to have landed outside the double bed in the second round of a World Matchplay game in Gibraltar versus Dean Winstanley (PDC said it was a 'rare human error' by the ref, Taylor subsequently offered to forfeit the game and give prize money to Winstanley, or to play a rematch).

Quote: 'Luke's emergence has been absolutely brilliant. I love the way he walks up there. He isn't interested in money. He's interested in titles. He's interested in enjoying himself. If he doesn't win, he isn't a sulker.' – on Luke Littler's rise

'You could hear a blob of vinegar drop on a chip in this hall.'

'He's twitching more than a one-legged ferret!'

YOU CAN'T BEAT A BIT OF BULLY

One of the greatest programmes ever shown on TV is back (again). This time, it's hosted by cricket legend Andrew 'Freddie' Flintoff, with darts players and quiz superstars looking to get through the tough early rounds to the final board, where they could hit the jackpot and win the big prize.

We speak, of course, of *Bullseye*. For people of a certain age, this cult show was must-see viewing on ITV in its 1980s and 1990s heyday, and looking back now on its mix of utterly crap prizes and absolutely unfashionable jumpers, it really is a time capsule that never fails to entertain.

It all began in 1981, first airing on Monday nights but soon moving to Sunday late afternoons on ITV. The basic format saw three teams of two – one 'thrower' and one 'knower' – competing against each other. Hosting was experienced comedian and compère Jim Bowen, whose patter and banter with the contestants was often unwittingly hilarious. He also had plenty of catchphrases: 'Super, smashing, great'; 'You can't beat a bit of Bully'; 'Keep out of the black and in the red, there's nothing in this game for two in a bed'. Bowen was a stalwart of working men's clubs and as such was a fairly unflappable host, if patronisingly sexist to women and holding some rather unreconstructed attitudes.

Format

Round one was all about the cash, with the darts players on the team looking to throw into a special board divided into categories (books, sport, showbiz, etc). The board was further divided into £10, £20 and £30 beds (the higher amounts closer to the bull and harder to hit). Once the darts player had hit a section with the single dart allowed, the knower had limited time to answer the attached question correctly. If a wrong category was hit, and the category had not previously been played, the question would still be asked but with no bonus money from the throw attached. A bullseye was worth £50. The amounts were later upped to £30, £50 and £100 (bull £200). The higher the score by the darts player, the more difficult that question too. Later series had an option for the other teams to buzz in if the question was answered incorrectly.

Initially at the end of round one the lowest-scoring team would be eliminated but in latter series all three teams went through to Pounds for Points – the second round. To a soundtrack of the jaunty theme tune, the darts players had one visit each to score as many points as possible. The team with the highest score got to answer the question, with a pound for each point. So, if the thrower got 180, there was £180 resting on that question. After three rounds of this, the lowest-scoring two teams were eliminated and the remaining team went through to Bully's Prize Board. Before that, though, it would be time for an ad break – just enough time for Jim to collect the two losing pairs, give them a tankard and a small toy Bully character, and for him to pull wads of cash out of his pockets, start counting it out and distributing it. That he looked like a dodgy nightclub promoter at the end of a cash-only pie-and-a-pint night was only part of the charm. While he did so, he'd exhort people to put the kettle on and come back for part two.

Chucking for charity

A celeb, usually a pro darts player, would have nine darts in total to try and score 301 or more. If they did, their total was doubled and cash to that amount donated by the programme to their chosen charity. If they scored less than 301, it was one pound per point. Under pressure, many pros went to pieces and couldn't get anywhere near the 301. It must be said, however, that strong rumours surrounded the show for years that the actual board was hung incorrectly; it was therefore not at the regulation height by some inches, which required huge adjustments from professionals and contestants alike.

Bully's Prize Board

This round is iconic for many reasons – firstly, as our Jim rightly pointed out, all the prizes were in six different numbered red zones around the board. The thrower had to successfully hit a particular zone to win the prize that Jim said was 'hiding behind it' – presuming the knower could answer the question correctly. Hitting the zone again, however, cancelled out that prize (the 'two in a bed' warning). Secondly, the prizes were even by 1980s standards, how can we put it? – *crap*. Yes, you might get a video recorder 'in one' (as scorer Tony Green would have it), but 'in two' might be something like a set of towels or a day out at Whipsnade Zoo. The bullseye here would provide 'Bully's Special Prize', which could be anything from a holiday in the Algarve to a new microwave oven (in the 1980s this was a huge prize). At the end of the prize board, the winning couple would have to decide whether to keep their prizes or to gamble them against Bully's Star Prize, about which they did not know. The cash was not at risk until that was changed in series 11 to give it more jeopardy. If the team decided not to go for the gamble but to take their prizes, the team in second place would be brought back and asked if they'd like to gamble instead, and likewise (but rarely) the chance would go right down to the team in last place.

Bully's Star Prize

Easy on paper, tough under pressure: six darts to get 101 or more. The non-darts player would go first, with a drum roll and suitably hushed audience ramping up the anxiety. The key always was for this player to ignore the 20 bed, and the attendant risks of hitting 1 or 5, and to simply aim for the left-hand side of the board. Anything approaching 40 or so was seen as a great start. The designated darts player would then hopefully mop up the remaining points to win the prize. As noted above, the variation in the board height was immensely unhelpful here and a surprising amount of skilled darts players went to pieces. Losing the gamble didn't just mean losing all your accumulated prizes (and later money), it also brought the dubious 'pleasure' of

Jim Bowen putting his arm around you and, while he intoned 'here's what you could have won', a section of the studio would reveal that star prize to all and sundry for the first time (including the audience).

The star prize

Bullseye is legendary for its barmy prizes. The real score was a car, something like a Ford Focus or other family runaround, which really was an excellent prize in those days. But it was all too often that (win or lose) Sunday-evening viewers would be falling about at the fact that a team from deepest Wolverhampton, miles from the sea, would have won . . . a speedboat. This iconic prize was so ludicrously inapt that it made a complete mockery of gambling in the first place. For a start, how the heck would they get it home? And after that, what would they do with it? Other prizes were holidays, a fitted kitchen (!!) and a bit more usefully, £5,000. The faces of the winners were often sadder than those of the losing gamblers at this point, making it a quintessentially British TV show that didn't quite break anyone out of their dismal day-to-day existence, but instead put them up there to bare their souls in front of millions of people, and at the end of it they'd go home with a completely inappropriate 'prize' while the credits rolled. Brilliantly, if the gamblers lost, the *Bullseye* theme would follow in a sad, minor key. Still, Jim Bowen would be his usual effervescent self, signing off with 'You can't beat a bit of Bully', and then going back to get all touchy-feely with the female contestants.

This isn't the first remake of the show – it was brought back in 2006 by Challenge TV with Dave Spikey at the helm. Spikey had a similar background to Bowen, although he was very much able to play it tongue-in-cheek, in common with the compère character he'd portrayed on the brilliant Peter Kay series about working men's clubs, *Phoenix Nights*. The prizes were miles better, but something wasn't quite the same, and after 30 episodes it was not renewed. The following year Vernon Kay presented a celebrity special, prompting rumours a decade later that he'd be in charge of another reboot in 2018. That didn't happen, but Alan Carr did present one episode in his *Epic Gameshow* series in July 2020.

And that brings us (nearly) up to date. ITV decided to commission a Christmas Special in 2024, with Freddie Flintoff as the host and Luke 'The Nuke' Littler on board as star player. The affable Lancastrian Flintoff had cultivated a TV career since retiring from cricket and is an avowed fan of both the original show and of course darts in general. He said that he couldn't 'quite believe I'll get to host this Christmas special' at the time so would have been over the moon when it was confirmed that a full series in 2025 was to follow.

Whether the new *Bullseye* will find its way to cult success is still up for grabs, but in our world of everything on air, all the time, everywhere, it's only a few clicks if you want to watch the highs and lows (and jumpers) of the original magnificent series. You really cannot beat a bit of Bully. *Mooooooo!*

'That was like throwing three pickled onions into a thimble.'

CAUGHT IN THE ACT

A day out at the darts has to be one of the greatest experiences known to mankind. Whether dressed up in a Pope Leo XIV suit or simply having it large with mates new and old, it's a perfect blend of sports appreciation and some adult beverages. Sadly, though, the time may come when you've already used all your holiday allocation, and so far at least six of your dear old grandmothers have been 'taken sick' in order that you can sleep off the excesses of a hefty night. Now, we do not condone pulling sickies by any means, but we're also realistic. There are cameras at the darts. You run the risk of being rumbled every time you stand up to cheer on another maximum from The Nuke, or dance along with Dimitri van den Bergh's latest disco extravaganza.

Here's what to do if your boss catches you on telly when you ought to be preparing spreadsheets and the presentation for the upcoming Dullard and Dullard Sporkstravaganza conference. We are in no way liable for any shenanigans that may ensue, so tread carefully. Some take a few months' preparation, but that golden prize is worth taking time to facilitate.

Plan one: The stick-on worker technique

How it works: You will have to decide on your darts costume well in advance, and take photos of you wearing it – preferably at the pub, or anywhere there's other revellers. Make these various photos into stickers, and place them surreptitiously where the boss will look: in picture frames around their office; in the corner of their computer screen; on the wing mirror of their car; on various advertisement hoardings on their usual route to work; in paperwork the boss will glance at. Essentially, everywhere their eyes might rest for a split second. Crucially, don't leave those photos there for ever. Once the boss has had a chance to clock them subconsciously, remove the pics. What we're doing here, in the great tradition of Derren Brown and his mates, is placing that shot of you into the mind of the boss. Ideally, they'll ask you 'Why are there pics of you everywhere?' – by which time you'll have removed them, so can genuinely reply, 'Where?' The confused boss will then look again at their executive desk tidy where they were convinced there was a shot of you – but there will not be one. You can tell them they need a holiday if they're spotting you everywhere, and they'll agree.

Hence, when they think they see you, all dressed up

and at the darts, they'll shake their heads because they've been primed for several months to see images of you all over the place – but also be convinced that it's all in their head.

Plan two: The flat-earth technique

How it works: Again, take time way before the darts championships to set this one up. The result we need here is to make the boss question whether there actually is a game called 'darts' at all. If you can involve other people in your work, rope them in to this one. When the boss is about, start conversations about 'watching the archery on telly' the previous evening, and instead of chatting about MVG's 170 checkout, talk about MVG's amazing bowstring technique. Pepper conversations with all the jargon of the archer, substituting arrowheads and taut pull-backs for chats about nine-darters. Come to work with a shirt featuring the image of Hawkeye or Robin Hood or Katniss Everdeen, giving them all the airtime you'd normally give to your memories of seeing Steve Beaton once try and charm his way to getting a free Bacardi and Coke down at Frimley Green.

With a fair wind behind you, your boss will see you at the darts, but because they're now convinced that there is no such sport at all, they'll shrug it off in favour of watching *The Green Arrow*, which you've helpfully downloaded for them onto a USB stick.

Plan three: The long-lost twin

How it works: Take a leaf out of the book of the writers of *Neighbours* and randomly start mentioning your identical twin brother or sister at every opportunity. Establish that they live miles away so you rarely see them. Make some blag photos of the two of you, together, at the beach/in the hot tub/caring for injured hedgehogs, and show the pics around the office. Then, when the World Championships are imminent, drop some hints that your long-lost sibling is likely to be in the country during that week. At the same time, cultivate an important 'client' (i.e. one of your mates) who you need to meet with in order to keep a potential deal bubbling away. Get your mate to come to your office – dressed in a suit and whatnot – and be sure the boss clocks the two of you chatting about actual work. Guess what? Your 'client' wants to meet up again . . . and it happens to be when the darts is on. Well, as a professional you must leave the office for this conflab. Indeed, this is reciprocal – you can do the same for your mate, in their own place of work, as they pull off this sleight-of-thought.

When the boss sees 'you' at the darts, something in the back of their mind will remind them that it's actually your identical twin enjoying the festivities, 'cause you're already out discussing contracts with your new client. Note that your 'client', if they also come with you to the darts, oughta wear something other than a business suit for maximum deniability.

Plan four: Wear a complete furry suit

How it works: Anything that involves a full-head covering will keep you safe – provided you don't take it off to have a drink. Yep, it's gonna get sweaty and minging. But you will keep your job.

Plan five: Invite the neighbours

How it works: Everyone knows that if you're gonna have a house party and things are gonna get a smidgin noisy as a result, the absolute best thing to do is to invite your neighbours in advance. Clearly this depends on getting on OK with the people who you share a street with, but it ain't half a great way to avoid any nastiness. So, if you get on well with your boss (and why wouldn't you?), start chatting about darts. If they're a fan, try and get the boss to designate a day out at the championships as a work event to raise morale and break the ice among the troops. You never know, the person in charge may have been trying to find ways of their own to get away with slipping out to cheer on Chizzy and co. for ages.

If all else fails, make sure you know of any upcoming job openings in your chosen field. You don't want to end up going viral like that dude in an unwise Christmas jumper did a year or two back . . .

'Keith Deller's not just an underdog, he's an underpuppy.'

'He's like Jack the Ripper on a Friday night.'

'That could have landed on the pupil of a fly's eyeball.'

'That's like giving Dracula the keys to the blood bank.'

ANSWERS

The Great Darts Players Challenge

1. b
2. a
3. b
4. a – he has joked over the years that competing against the likes of Phil Taylor sped up his hair loss, but in reality it's just a natural process
5. b – it's been repeated so often in the press that if it was originally a joke it's now accepted as truth. This is the modern world, folks. Luke is a Leeds fan, though
6. a
7. c
8. a – Sherrock went on to beat Mensur Suljović 3–1 in the next round but lost 4–2 to Chris Dobey in the next round
9. b – yes, The Asp could have been playing professional footy, had things gone a little different
10. c – he eventually fessed up about it

11. a
12. b – though he is based in England
13. a
14. a
15. b – though a is also, of course, true
16. c – not only that, he hit four other ton-plus outs during the match, which he won 4–3 in an all-time classic
17. c
18. a
19. b
20. a
21. a
22. b
23. a – yes, folks, that's what we call Top Bantz
24. a
25. a
26. b – 13 at the time of writing. What can you do?
27. a – yes, the great Gerwyn Price. He even scored a try for Cross Keys in the 2012 WRU Challenge Cup Final!
28. b – he said earplugs didn't drown out the noise (and the booing). The PDC quickly amended their regulations to ban over-the-ear headphones or ear defenders. Price lost the quarter-final match to Gabriel Clemens (5–1) in any case
29. c
30. a
31. c – a beautiful, beautiful train at that, built in 1923 and authenticated as reaching 100mph in 1934. Yes, let's

remember that when the 20:21 to Aldershot is stuck in a siding for 68 minutes due to the wrong kind of fuggin' leaves on the line

32. c
33. a
34. b
35. b
36. a – and we wish Dimitri all the very best health
37. b
38. c
39. a – Gotta catch 'em all!
40. b – ah, come on, it's a *good joke*
41. a
42. c
43. b – a camera crew later gave him the broken pieces of the glass trophy back, in a cardboard box
44. a
45. c
46. c
47. b
48. b
49. a
50. b – Derek Dick is the real name of Fish of Marillion fame, ladies and gents. Use that in your next pub quiz, and if you win money, send us 10 per cent please, ta

Darts 101

1. a
2. b
3. c
4. b
5. a
6. b. 21 – 1 to 20, plus single bull (the one which doesn't show how much it's worth – 25)
7. c – but please don't get in a situation where b applies
8. b – but don't do a. either
9. b
10. a
11. a
12. a – the inner ring trebles the score, i.e. treble 20
13. b: single 16 means you're left with D8; single 8 = D4; S4 = D2; S2 = D1
14. b
15. c
16. a
17. b
18. c – notionally, because it's impossible to 'escape' from D1. Every other double, if you hit a single instead, has an alternative finishing route available
19. a
20. c – and we hope you hear it very, very often with the help of this book!

On the Oche

1. b. Also accept: 2.93 metres from the same origin
2. a. This even applies to aliens from the planet Zog, who may have more than two feet, and octopuses must consider tentacles as feet for the purposes of this quiz
3. b, d, e and f are all cited. Note that researchers have never found an actual brewer called S. Hockey and Sons – but for our purposes it is a possible origin story too. There are also probably loads more, but we're concentrating on these six for our quiz. There's an interesting shout that maybe it's something to do with the sport of hockey, too

The History of Darts

1. b – of course, there will be proto-darts games before this. The Romans, for example, may have used sharpened sticks with feathers to hit targets; basically anywhere you find soldiers, sharp projectiles and downtime you'll find some kind of ancient game with some kind of relationship to darts
2. a
3. b – the fairground-stall game of throwing a prototype dart at some kind of board, with different sections labelled for scores or prizes, has been around for centuries
4. b – however, we have tried to corroborate this and can only find one unreferenced source, folks. If you have any more info, please do let us know

5. c – Henry VIII, in other words. Given he was an extremely skilled and avid sportsman in his youth and renowned for his vigour, it makes sense that he'd enjoy a game of darts (and the ale that went with it, no doubt). He only became the fat, very grumpy weirdo in that famous portrait after enduring a painful jousting injury to his leg, which went septic and caused pain for the rest of his life

6. a – again, however, provenance is a bit sketchy. There was also a chap named Thomas William Buckle who was by trade a dartboard maker. He definitely made the Yorkshire Board variant, and according to some sources also standardised the modern (London) board. If anyone names him, give 'em a point in ol' Bucko's honour

7. c – it was important that it was not considered a game of chance, because that would mean darts was about gambling, which was prohibited

8. b – no relation to Skywalker, or indeed his nemesis – Dart Vader

9. c – some sources also cite 1924 so a point for either answer

10. a

11. a

12. b

13. a – some sources quote 1962 because a Westward TV Invitational was held, but they're wrong :) Technically, it was a test transmission from BBC Indoor Games and featuring presenters Jasmine Bligh and Leslie Mitchell – so a woman got there first for a change. Darts was also on the radio – the mind

boggles as to how that one worked out – with a listing for a match in a 1937 broadcast in Northern Ireland

14. b – amazing to think that the newspaper itself no longer exists. It was a Sunday gossip-type tabloid, which closed down after many shenanigans were brought to light. We won't go into that here for legal reasons, but it's a heck of a story in itself

15. b

16. c

17. b

18. c – Eric Bristow wasn't a fan, saying it 'didn't do the sport any favours' to present darts players as fat drinkers. To be fair, there always used to be at least one pint on show for players in those days onstage, believe it or not

19. b

20. c

Anatomy of a Dart

1. a – also accept 'tip' for 'point' and 'shaft' for 'stem'. No giggling at the back

2. b

3. c

4. If a player's dart fulfils any of these three points, they are not permitted for competition use as they fall outside the DRA's specifications

5. a. If the match ref deems them as being damaging to the board, they will not be permitted as this will be to the disadvantage of the opponent/s

6. c – a foul throw is called otherwise
7. a – in varying amounts and not necessarily including all three elements. If you've said c) you're in *Star Trek*, so get to the Holodeck immediately and call up the 'after midnight' program featuring Seven of Nine, Counsellor Troi and a paddling pool full of warm custard
8. The tip retracts a touch into the barrel when it impacts on the board. This helps to get rid of any bounce-outs because the forwards force of the dart continues a little after the dart tip hits the board. This means more mass is available to push the dart into the board, hence more force can be retained from the throwing action. Isaac Newton described this in his first law of motion, but we didn't listen properly in school so we can't quote it here
9. a – a soft-tip dart is just that – the tip/point is usually plastic and while much less damaging than steel-tipped ones can still be extremely sharp. So, y'know, don't chuck 'em at each other's eyes. Though you can technically use them with bristle boards, and there are also some non-electronic soft-tip specified boards, they are most often used with electronic dartboards. The board's sensors log where the darts land, and calculate your score. Some boards can also give you suggested finishes, tell you the scores out loud, shout 'one hundred and EIIIIGHTTTYYYYY' and give you a happy ending to every game. As in, make sure everyone ends up enjoying themselves playing darts. What? *Ahem*. Anyway, another advantage of electronic darts is that, technically, as the board logs each dart's position, that

information can be supplied near-instantly worldwide, meaning virtual reconstructions of matches are possible
10. a
11. b – the name of a Japanese soft-tip darts company
12. c – in 2013, 2016 and 2017. Lim was invited to the PDC Worlds after his 2013 success, and qualified for the following year's PDC Worlds due to his high-ranking position in DARTSLIVE
13. c
14. b – but it must be with the express prior knowledge of the tournament director/match ref before the match begins, and obviously they have to adhere to all rules, weights, lengths and so on. You can also repair your throwing equipment at the discretion of the ref
15. b – only if it's dropped before the player has begun the deliberate action of a throw. In other words, once you're lining it up and aiming, if it leaves your hand it's counted as a throw. If it slips out of your hand at any other time then it's legitimately a dropped dart not in play so can be retrieved and used. Bounce-outs are dead darts – sorry
16. b – nothing – you've already won once 'game shot' has been called, so the game is technically over. Don't do it, though, 'cause if you knock out a wobbly winner, your opponent is likely to protest that your winning dart would have fallen out of its own accord (rendering it an invalid dart) and you'll have a right old kerfuffle
17. c

18. a – when the darts collide with each other, tiny invisible little nicks and scratches can develop, and this affects the aerodynamic and parabolic performance of the projectile. When you're working with such incredibly tight margins as the very top players are, this can be the difference between a successful throw and, say, a wire-affected bounce-out. These are miniscule variations, but that's the game, folks
19. b – and they're loads of fun but absolute pigs to chuck
20. c – benign though it might seem, it turns out that chucking big things of about a foot in length around that have pointy ends can be a bit sketchy. Thousands of injuries and several deaths have been attributed to lawn darts and in the US and Canada, and you can no longer buy pointy-tipped lawn darts. We really worry for the lads in Bros on this one

Who Said It?

'I am on a fat-free diet for most of the year, but before The Worlds I tend to relax on the diet a bit to concentrate on darts.' – Phil Taylor

'I'd missed the boat in rugby, I was stuck in a rut and I needed a change. I was lucky to have darts as an option.' – Gerwyn Price

'All this cuddling and kissing on stage these days, well it's all right in football when someone scores a goal, but not when

you're playing darts.' – Eric Bristow
'I always wear flat shoes for darts because a heel can put me off balance.' – Adrian Lewis

'I've beaten two of the best players in the world, and if that doesn't say that women can't play darts I don't know what can.' – Fallon Sherrock

'I can offer my family things that I could never have dreamed of – darts has changed my life.' – Rob Cross

'I got into darts from watching it on TV, and I used to joke with my friends: "I could do that, I could be the best in the world." I told them I'd be the world champion.' – John Part

'If I look at the standard of darts on TV, I think I have taken it to a new level.' – Michael van Gerwen

'I don't have any GCSEs, everyone probably has more than me. Although I did pass my sport.' – Luke Littler

'Lucky I'm an old man now. When I was younger I would have won the handsome stakes hands down.' – Bobby George

Can You Hit the Bullseye?

1. a – often referred to as 'bristle boards'. If it's c then you've got problems, folks

2. Cork; (coiled) paper; wood; plastic; metal (for magnetic darts) – others may exist, so if someone insists on a different material, and can back it up with a quick search from *two* independent sources, give 'em a point (or take one away for being annoying)
3. b – aka Sisal, from the *Agave sisalana* plant. Sometimes called sisal hemp (not that kind of hemp, you fiends)
4. a – 17 ¾ inches, though you *may* see 18 inches
5. c – 1.5 inches
6. b – the wires themselves are often thinner too
7. a
8. The tournament director can do it whenever they wish; players/team captains can request a change, and the referee or designated official can consider their request. The opponent/ opposing captain can object, and the final decision goes to the tournament director. So, basically, anyone can ask but only the tourney boss can actually do it
9. b – *but* leniency is also allowed and the DRA's exact wording allows also for 'at the next suitable break in play' – effectively if the board's visibly knackered it could happen straight away, but you're unlikely to see this at the world level
10. c

What's in a name?

Adam Hunt – The Hunter
Adrian Lewis – Jackpot

Alan Norris – Chuck
Anastasia Dobromyslova – From Russia With Love
Andrew Gilding – Goldfinger
Andy Boulton – X-Factor
Bob Anderson – The Limestone Cowboy
Bobby George – Bobby Dazzler
Brendan Dolan – Historymaker
Ceri Morgan – The Hulk
Chris Dobey – Hollywood
Colin Osbourne – Ozzy
Damon Heta – The Heat
Danny Noppert – The Freeze
Daryl Gurney – Superchin
Dave Chisnall – Chizzy
Dennis Priestley – The Menace
Dimitri van den Bergh – The Dreammaker
Dirk van Duijvenbode – Titan
Dylan Slevin – Oceans
Eric Bristow – The Crafty Cockney
Fallon Sherrock – Queen of the Palace
Gabriel Clemens – The German Giant
Gary Anderson – Flying Scotsman
Gerwyn Price – The Iceman
Jamie Lewis – Fireball
Jan Dekker – Double Dekker
Jeffrey de Graaf – The Rebel
Jelle Klaasen – The Cobra

Joe Cullen – The Rock Star
John Lowe – Old Stoneface
John Part – Darth Maple
Jonny Clayton – The Ferret
José de Sousa – The Special One
Josh Rock – Rocky
Kai Gotthardt – The Tunnel
Keane Barry – Dynamite
Kevin Doets – Hawkeye
Kevin Painter – The Artist
Kim Huybrechts – The Hurricane
Krzysztof Ratajski – The Polish Eagle
Leighton Rees – Marathon Man
Luke Humphries – Cool Hand Luke
Luke Littler – The Nuke
Madars Razma – Latvian Razzmatazz
Mark Webster – Spider
Martin Adams – Wolfie
Matt Campbell – Ginja Ninja
Max Hopp – Maximiser
Michael Smith – Bully Boy
Michael van Gerwen – Mighty Mike
Mike De Decker – The Real Deal
Mitchell Clegg – The Moosta
Nathan Aspinall – The Asp
Paul Lim – The Singapore Slinger
Peter Wright – Snakebite

Phil Taylor – The Power
Raymond van Barneveld – Barney
Ricardo Pietreczko – Pikachu
Richie Burnett – The Prince of Wales
Ricky Evans – Rapid
Ritchie Edhouse – Madhouse
Rob Cross – Voltage
Ronnie Baxter – The Rocket
Ross Smith – Smudger
Ryan Joyce – Relentless
Ryan Searle – Heavy Metal
Scott Rand – Cool Hand
Scott Williams – Shaggy
Simon Whitlock – The Wizard
Stephen Bunting – The Bullet
Stephen Burton – Bertie
Steve Beaton – The Bronzed Adonis
Trina Gulliver – Golden Girl
Wayne Mardle – Hawaii 501
William O'Connor – The Magpie

Red Herrings (i.e. we made them up):
Carlton Wuck – The Phenomenon
Robbie Diebel – The 12-Year-Old Vintage
Rocky Mademann – Hellraiser

It's All About the Board

1. a
2. b
3. c
4. b – numerous others were used after the 1970s when Dutch elm disease decimated elm stocks, so award a discretionary point for good disease knowledge
5. a – by some mad genius at Harrows, if you want to be exact
6. b
7. L: London 5s, R: Ipswich 5s (Ipswich 5s are also known as 'wide 5s'); the double and treble beds of the Ipswich/Wide 5s are, well, wider; games begin with scores of 505
8. a
9. a
10. a

Whose Injury?

Peter Wright – gallstones
Nathan Aspinall – hole in wrist tendon
Jelle Klaasen – tendonitis in wrist
Simon Whitlock – rolled ankle due to being jumped on by Adam Smith-Neale
Adam Smith-Neale – broken leg
Alan Warriner-Little – neck injury
Darius Labanauskas – pierced finger in left hand due to catching bounce-out
Luke Littler – stung by wasp

Jermaine Wattimena – injured index finger in non-throwing hand due to ham carving injury on Christmas Day
Kim Huybrechts – double fracture of collarbone in Belgian Cup Final fans' dust-up
Michael van Gerwen – neck injury after putting shirt on wrongly
Gary Anderson – shoulder injury due to cutting down trees

Nine-Dart Heroes

1. c
2. T20, T19, D12; T20, T15, D18; T19, T16, D18; T17, T18, D18
3. T20, T19, bullseye x3
4. T20, T17, D15
5. a
6. b
7. c
8. c
9. c – in the MFI World Matchplay, 13 October, 1984. It was recorded for later broadcast
10. a, b, and c – possibly the most serious-looking dart hero of all time

One Hundred and Eiiiiiiiiighty

1. c – but you must go second, as follows: leg one, player one throws first – both players throw 180; both players throw 180 again; player one then hits the 141 checkout for a nine-darter

and player two does not use their visit as a consequence. Leg two – same again, but player two throws first this leg. Both score 180 on their first and second visits, therefore player two has thrown four in a row, while player one has 'only' managed two in a row because of the 141 finish on their third visit to win leg one

2. a. – as per the above it's four scores in four visits of 180 over two legs; so 4 x 3 treble twenties = 12 darts used. Then also add the next two darts of the final visit by player two in their own third visit with 141 remaining and you've got 14 maximums in a row. Note that this would be a very silly thing to do because when on 141 if you score 120 (two maximums) you ruin your nine-darter by leaving 21 – not a double – and can't finish. For those reasons you are way more likely to see seven treble 20s in a row in this context from player one, and 13 in a row from player two (or 6/12 if they choose a different way around the finish on their third visit, to finish)

3. c

4. a

5. b – he is also Welsh, which is obviously to his great credit, but not the answer we're after here, *mae'n ddrwg gennym ni*

6. c – on Yorkshire TV's *Indoor League*

7. a

8. b – must be something in the water down that way

9. a

10. c

11. c

12. a, b, and c. But the most useful answer is b

Darts On Screen and in Fiction

1. Martin Amis: *London Fields*
2. c
3. b
4. b
5. a
6. b
7. b – *Heiko's World* in English (accept either answer)
8. b
9. a – and you're welcome for the earworm
10. c

Walk-On Music (players' songs quiz)

1. a. Luke Littler
b. James Wade
c. Dimitri van den Bergh

2. a. Michael van Gerwen
b. Ross Smith
c. Michael Smith

3. a. Ryan Searle
b. Dave Chisnall
c. Peter Wright

4. a. Gary Anderson
b. Nathan Aspinall
c. Luke Littler

5. a. Martin Schindler
b. Joe Cullen
c. Mike De Decker

CREDITS AND ACKNOWLEDGEMENTS

Thanks to Joe '180' Hallsworth for seeing this one through from the very first tentative Q-School steps to the final nine-darter; Suzy and the boys as ever; Bangor City 1876. *Sdim eisiau esgus i gael amser dda.*

This project was researched, written and delivered without any generative AI or Large Language Models at any stage. It's just a fuggin' posh text-prediction system, folks. Anyone who puts this text in a position to be stolen by scrapers of Gen AI is a poo-head, a crumbled egg and a small-minded thief, and I hope someone comes into your house and pisses in your kettle.

Join – and use – your local library. They don't come back once they're gone.

No human is illegal. We are all from immigrant stock eventually. Yes, even you, mate. Grow up.

Trans rights are human rights. Solidarity and love.